A YEAR IN THE GARDEN

MOLLY HACKETT

&

GEORGIANNA TAYLOR

D1616402

A YEAR IN THE GARDEN

MOLLY HACKETT & GEORGIANNA TAYLOR

Copyright 2001
by
Molly Hackett
&
Georgianna Taylor

Library of Congress Control Number 2001094747

ISBN 1-931291-08-X

Published in the United States of America

STONEYDALE PRESS PUBLISHING COMPANY
523 Main Street • P.O. Box 188
Stevensville, Montana 59870
Phone: 406-777-2729

Table of Contents

Cover Photos: *The photographs on the cover were taken by Ellyn P. Jones. Left row, top to bottom, radishes, poppies, green tomatoes, foxgloves; center, lettuce and double bloodroot; right row, apple, zucchini blossoms, and a shade garden in the spring.*

INTRODUCTION

We western Montana gardeners are special.

Our gardens and flowerbeds must be the horticultural equivalent of the hardy frontiersmen and their tough and resilient women. We just don't have a comfortable niche in the texts and popular gardening manuals published on the East and West Coasts. Those don't give much attention to places that have a few June days tucked into the middle of February or receive snowstorms in May. Our weather is special, our dirt is different and our gardeners especially determined.

The two of us decided to write about gardening out of our own frustration. All the gardening books we could find were written for somewhere else. They assumed frost-free seasons of nine months instead of three. They assumed winters with reliable snow cover to insulate perennial plants and minimum temperatures comfortably above zero. They explained how to care for flowers and vegetables that thrive 200 or 300 miles south of where we were trying to garden. They gave no consideration to a climate where gardens exist only with regular irrigation.

We decided it was time for us to share our mistakes and our triumphs with the other gardeners who inhabit this exceptional part of the planet. Since we had learned through so much trial and still more error, perhaps we could help shorten the road to successful gardens for others.

In 1991 we began a newspaper column composed of questions we had been asked and new gardening developments we had learned. We have made every effort to respect our readers, to keep a light touch and never to take ourselves too seriously.

Having found our best successes through painful, hands-on experience, we have reservations about the advice of "experts" without such experience. We adopted as our motto, "Never trust a gardener with clean fingernails," and named the column "Dirty Fingernails." We wear our grimy hands as a badge of pride and when in polite company simply hide them behind our backs.

Response to the column was immediate and our area of coverage has expanded from the Bitterroot Valley to include the rest of Western Montana. Our first book, *The Compleat Gardener,* published in 1995, is a distillation of the questions and answers in our first four years of columns. With the wider distribution available to a book, it soon became apparent that the questions from our newspaper readers were common to gardeners in many other areas of the country. Feedback indicated that the answers and advice originally given to Western Montanans also were applicable throughout the northern United States.

This book is dedicated to the gardeners who ask the questions, wherever they may be. We all are part of the same gardening fraternity, whether young or old, novice or veteran. Some readers will see their questions or their comments in these pages. We all learn from each other, and this book is one more way to pass help and advice from gardener to gardener. It is another link in the connection among all those who cherish plants and the growing of plants for their beauty, for food, for the challenge and for the magic of watching it all happen.

Spring

SPRING

Q: I have some old-fashioned roses that are too tall — the blooms are all way up in the air. Is it safe to cut out some of those big old canes?

A: Yes, indeed. Not just safe, but desirable, and spring is a good time to do it. Not only will you get those roses down where you can see and smell them, you will have more blossoms. They bloom better on younger wood.

It would be perfectly safe to cut half the canes out this year and half next year. You can cut them right down to ground level. This will give you a Mutt and Jeff-looking plant this summer, but by next year it should be completely rejuvenated.

The rose probably will not bloom on its new growth this year, although you may get a few flowers late in the summer if yours is an ever-blooming variety. Most old-fashioned roses bloom best on two-year-old wood.

To keep the bush shapely, go in every year or two and cut out any cane that is getting too straggly or tall. What you really want to do is encourage it to make a lot of new growth.

Q: Can you give me some advice about planting trees around my new house?

A: Here is the latest information to give you the best possible chance for success. One might as well be up-to-date, although the experts keep changing their minds with amazing regularity.

Unless you need to plant bigger trees to provide a screen immediately, plant small trees. A three-foot tree is going to grow better, on average, than any tree larger than that. Small trees are young, physiologically, and therefore are more adaptable — better able to stand change. They get themselves adjusted to their new place more quickly, they grow fast and before long will have passed up trees that were bigger when planted at the same time.

Bare root trees do better than container trees, but they must be planted while still dormant — before all the nursery specimens are leafing out.

Arguments about spring vs. fall planting go on and on. Right now the spring planting experts are way ahead. We always have preferred planting our trees in spring, so we agree with these particular experts.

First figure out spacing. How close should your new tree be to a building and other trees and shrubs? Deal with how big it is going to be and not how big it is now.

Dig the hole wide and shallow, just deep enough for the roots to fit, but wide enough to spread the roots nicely. That's entirely different from what we learned twenty years ago. In 1987 some good research was done and everybody believed the results enough that they all latched onto it, and it has become accepted practice.

Do not add anything to improve the soil when you plant a tree. Research on that, reported in 1993, showed that soil improvements do not help the tree establish itself or stay alive. They simply waste money. If the tree is not going to live in the soil you have without improvement, you need to find a different spot to plant it.

When you improve soil in a hole, the tree grows fast until its roots fill up the hole, but then they just go around in a circle as if they are in a plastic pot and don't grow out into the unimproved soil. The tree grows fine for about five years, then starts looking worse and worse and just dies.

If you haven't already set your heart on a particular kind of tree to plant, you might like to know that those with fibrous roots, like mountain ash, do better than those with coarse roots, like oak. That is especially true of bigger trees.

DO NOT LET THE ROOTS GET DRY DURING THE PLANTING PROCEDURE – EVEN FOR FIVE MINUTES.

If you do, the tree may well die. It is perfectly OK to dig the hole days ahead of time if you want to, so you can bring the tree home and poke it right in the ground. A bare root tree will be fine for several hours the way you brought it from the nursery. If you take it out of the wet sawdust, or whatever it's in, you can stand it in a bucket of water while getting the hole ready.

Plant the tree at the same level it was at in the nursery. It is very important not to plant it deeper. If you do, it may die, and even if it doesn't, it never will grow as well. Trees know where the soil line was and don't appreciate someone trying to tell them it was somewhere else.

There are very few cases where you want to stake a tree – this is another case where the advice has changed. They used to say it was important to stake so the tree wouldn't move around too much in the wind. They have discovered that as long as the root ball doesn't move around, it's fine for the tree to move. It will increase the diameter of its trunk faster from learning to deal with the wind and end up being a sturdier tree.

There still is no consensus as to whether you should use anti-transpirants or the polymers you put in the soil to hold water. This choice is all yours.

Weeding around a tree is very important, as is keeping grass away until the tree is well established. If you take off a circle of sod four or five feet in diameter, that is a good size to keep weed – and grass – free until the new tree is growing well.

To make the job easier, you can lay down landscape cloth in that circle and cover it with bark. There are some paper ground covers that will biodegrade after a year or two. If you use a plastic one, be sure to take it off within a couple of years or you will be sorry. Grass and weeds grow up through it and down through it and it will take three strong men and a small boy to get it up.

Irrigation is vital. If you have clay soil, be careful not to drown the tree. Otherwise, the bigger problem will be to keep it wet enough. Check soil moisture very frequently for at least the first few weeks and prepare to water your new tree more than anything else in your landscape for the first season. You want it to grow lots of roots and not to be water-stressed at all in its first year. Water stress is easy to come by around here.

During the first growing season, prune only dead wood and do not fertilize at all for the first year.

Q: You keep talking about mulch. What is mulch, anyway?

A: There are two different kinds – organic and inorganic. They do two different things. Inorganic plastic mulches are used to warm the soil in the spring. The opaque ones – black or dark brown – can also be used in vegetable gardens, cutting a slit or X where you are going to plant a seedling. This will suppress the weeds, but the problem is that the plastics are impermeable, and you need a drip irrigation system which you lay before putting down the plastic.

There is a special purpose plastic covered with pinholes so it can be used with sprinkler irrigation. There are also ones called IRT, for infra-red transmitting. They are mostly dark green; they will keep down weeds, but they also provide extra heat, the way clear plastic does. Water does not get through them.

Landscape cloth of various constructions is not strictly a mulch. It is designed as a weed suppressant in decorative plantings and is usually covered with bark, chips or rock. Some special mulches, like plastics in different colors, are being tested to see if they will increase vegetable yields. A red one seems to produce more tomatoes and some foil ones reflect extra light to fruits. The final word is not in on any of those.

Organic mulches are used in both vegetable and small fruit gardens, in flowerbeds and around shrubs and trees – all kinds of plantings. An organic mulch can be made of anything that once was alive – grass, chopped weeds, compost, ground bark, chopped bark, sawdust, paper. If you are going to use the weeds you pull up, be sure you get them before they make seeds.

Sometimes organic mulches are used just for decorative effect, but they are good weed suppressants and important conservers of water. Bare soil will evaporate about twice as much water as soil covered with a good mulch.

Organic mulches do not raise the soil temperature – they actually make it cooler – so it is important not to put them on until after the soil has warmed up. Once the weather gets hot, mulch is useful to keep roots cool. Container plants suffer when their roots get too hot and will survive better if well mulched in the heat.

Trees and shrubs often are given a permanent organic mulch that can be up to four inches deep. This will keep grass competition away, as well as doing the other things mulch does.

There are also things called living mulches. Experiments have been done in the last several years with plants being planted among hairy vetch, but only that one variety of vetch. Most of the information has come from other parts of the country and we don't think there is enough evidence yet to warrant adopting it here on a big scale.

Planting annuals around other flowers that like cool roots, such as clematis or lilies, can be considered a living mulch. One important benefit of organic mulches is that they improve the soil as they break down. The more woody the stuff you mulch with, the less nutrient value it has, but any mulch as it breaks down provides humus and helps the texture of the soil. The coarser the pieces, the slower it breaks down and the slower the nutrients are released.

The final advantage to mulch is that whenever you cover bare soil with mulch, you don't have to till it and when you don't till, you are not bringing up the weed seeds.

Q: Can I use sawdust from a lumber mill to mulch my ferns so they don't dry out? Someone told me the turpentine wasn't good for plants and that it would hurt the nitrogen.

A: Your source has a couple of different ideas combined there. It is not the turpentine that can cause a problem. People do worry about nitrogen loss with the use of fresh organic materials, but turpentine doesn't do it.

It takes the bacteria in the soil to break down the sawdust into compost. They need nitrogen to break down the wood fiber. The idea is that they will take nitrogen from the soil that would normally go to the plants and use it to break down sawdust instead and that only after this is done will nitrogen be available for the plants.

As far as we know, there is some truth in that, but it is only true if you mix the sawdust into the soil because the good bugs only hang out down there in the dark.

Some fairly careful testing has shown that it is safe to put sawdust on top as a mulch. It will take it a very long time to turn into compost, but it's not going to take nitrogen from your ferns in the process.

Q: Can I use lawn clippings treated with weed killers as mulch?

A: We don't know of any studies on mulching specifically, but there has been research done in Minnesota, Oregon and Ohio on compost. We think the answers would be the same for mulch.

What the researchers found out was that you do need to worry, but only for a little while.

Evidently, you need wait only for the period of time that the container of herbicide tells you to wait for seed germination or planting new plants. If says, "wait a week," or "wait two weeks before planting again," wait that long before you use it as mulch or put it in your compost.

The breakdown rate varies a little with the temperature, moisture content and soil type, but the directions will err on the side of caution. Those companies don't want anyone killing off new plants with their product because of not waiting long enough. If you follow the container directions, you should be perfectly safe.

Q: I have a lot of pine needles. Can I use them for mulch on my flowerbeds? If I do, will it make the soil acid?
What about mulching with wood ashes? Are there mulches I can put on in winter that won't have to be taken off in the spring?

A: You certainly can use pine needles on anything you want. They won't make the soil acid enough to make much difference and they have the distinct advantage of hanging together and not blowing away like leaves every time a front goes through. You would have to put on a mountain of mulch to change your soil's pH significantly. In addition, pine needles decompose so slowly that any acid they have is released over a long period. In the third place, neither the rain that falleth from the skies nor the water that cometh from your sprinkler is acid, so it will neutralize any acid you might put into the soil. That's why it takes such determined and persistent effort to keep an acid soil here.

Do NOT use wood ashes. The reason the books recommend them is because the books were written by people living in areas with acid soil, which is not here. Wood ashes are NOT good for our soil. Period. You can create really serious problems with wood ashes in gardens around here.

As for mulches you won't have to remove, you can use anything organic that will break down fairly quickly. An easy mulch to create is chopped up stems of the plants the frost has just killed. Chopped weeds are fine as long as they aren't seeded out. Grass clippings are excellent, but you must let them dry out a few days (maybe one day if it is really sunny) so they don't form an impenetrable mat. Clippings dry faster if you spread, rather than pile, them. In a pile, they are likely to mold.

Compost, if you have it to spare, makes a great mulch.

All those things break down quickly and by the time you are ready to plant in the spring, you probably won't recognize much of the stuff you put on in the fall.

Even mulches that don't break down can be left on, as long as they are not in a place where you need to turn the soil. Around trees, shrubs and perennial beds you can use any mulch that is attractive, like chopped bark. During the growing season, mulches conserve moisture, and keep the soil cool on a hot afternoon.

Q: What kind of manure is the best fertilizer?

A: Historically, there actually are fertilizer fashions. For instance, the period when cars were first beginning to come into use was a period of high fashion in horse manure, presumably because it was the most available. Urban people got quite upset when cars took the horses out of the city because horse manure was the only thing you could possibly put on a garden. Horticulture would be ruined.

There have been periods when sheep manure was fashionable and when pig manure was in style. The funniest thing, however, was an ad from 1900 that offered canary guano as being the best fertilizer in the world. It must have been like harvesting saffron threads. Pound for pound it was worth as much as potted dahlias!

Q: I have been hearing quite a lot about "extending the season" and would like to try it in my garden. What would you recommend for starters in this area?

A: Floating row covers are the best thing for gardening since sliced tomatoes. They are made from nonwoven, manmade fibers which admit light. They come five or six feet wide and are available at area garden centers or through gardening specialty catalogs.

They are available in three different weights. Medium weight can be used for everything – as a frost protector spring and fall, or for protection from insects. This weight will give your plants four or five degrees more warmth than ambient air temperature. Heavy weight is good for seven or eight degrees.

The lightest weight does not provide frost protection but is great as a summer season bug protector. It is especially good for prevention of root maggots that eat up your onions and radishes, and for cabbage worms. These pests don't crawl up to your vegetables. They are hatched on the plants from eggs laid on them by a small fly in the case of root maggots and by white butterflies in the case of cabbage worms. If you keep the winged creatures off, you won't have to worry about their larvae eating or ruining your crop. If you grow your broccoli under a row cover, you won't have to fret about finding a cooked green worm garnishing your dinner plate.

You can grow things under covers of both the light and medium weight for the entire season. The heavy weight is great for spring. You can grow things under it for a month or six weeks, but eventually you do have to take it off because it cuts down enough available light that the plants start getting tall and scrawny. Also, since it takes a pretty heavy rain to get through, you will have to water under the cover.

The lightest weight can float directly on the plants, but the medium and heavy weights need a hoop of wire or PVC pipe to hold them up off the plants. Make hoop tunnels three to four feet across on the bottom and space rows of hoops about three feet apart.

There are several ways to hold down the row covers. One is oversized staples made of old coat hangers or other heavy wire. Make them an inch wide and about six inches long. Put a wad of the material under them, rather than poking them through the fabric to avoid having them tear in the wind.

If you make a long tunnel, you can lay a board along the edge, or you can weigh the edges down with rocks or even shovel a little dirt over the fabric edge.

At this time of year, you can make a tunnel and start your early garden as much as a month earlier than you normally would.

Your garden season can be extended by covering individual plants with hot caps or milk jugs, which provide about as much protection as light or medium weight row covers or any plastic. If you use milk jugs, you have to be sure to take the lids off when it's warm or you will boil the plants in their own juice.

The absolute best thing short of a greenhouse is walls of water. The homemade equivalent is water-filled plastic bottles put around plants. We haven't tried that, but we have used walls of water, which have been tested to 15 degrees. Both of us have had plants survive perfectly well with the water frozen solid in the tubes. Don't count on starting your plants more than a month early in a wall of water because within a month the plant will probably have grown out the top.

You can use plastic covers, but they provide only as much insulation as the lightest weight row covers, a couple of degrees. You also have to be around during the day so you can roll them up as soon as the sun comes out. Plastic covers are really not as practical in this climate where we have such extremes of temperature.

Plastic is easy to handle – you can build a frame and cover and move it around, a sort of portable cold frame. It has wonderful light transmission, but you need to use care because it heats up underneath very quickly.

Plastic is wonderful, lying flat on the ground, to warm up soil. That lets you plant earlier because one of the things that really slows down the vegetable garden is soil too cold for the seed to germinate. The seed sits there and rots instead of sprouting.

You can use either black or clear plastic. The advantage to black is that the weeds won't germinate under it. The soil warms up faster under clear plastic, but you get a whole forest of weed seedlings.

Plastic is great for cold frames, which can be made with hoops or with walls of boards, cinder blocks or straw bales. Covers for cold frames often are made of old storm windows with plastic stapled on instead of glass. To get more insulating value, staple plastic on both sides of the window frame so you get a dead air layer to hold in the heat.

If you are going to use plastic, buy something that is ultraviolet resistant, or plan to replace it twice a year – at this altitude it may not last a whole season without treatment.

A problem we don't always think about at this time of year is wind. Wind is really hard on plants because when a plant is windblown, it closes up the stomata (pores) on its leaves and can't breathe. This makes it impossible for the plant to grow well or to photosynthesize. It can end up being permanently stunted.

So you might want to think about putting up a windbreak – something temporary like shade cloth or plastic wind fence, or permanent plantings of shrubs. Clear plastic fastened to fence posts is not really efficient. The best material is something that lets through 50 percent of the wind. With total wind blocking you get eddies that are actually stronger than the steady winds.

Q: What on earth does it mean when the seed catalog says a variety of cucumbers is gynoecious?

A: It may sound rather poisonous, but it isn't. It just means the cucumbers are hybrids that produce plants with female flowers. Since most cucumber plants must be pollinated to produce fruit, seeds for gynoecious plants will be packaged with a few seeds for some variety that produces male seeds. They look the same, so unless you plant them all, you can't be sure you are sowing some of each. Don't use them if you plan to grow only one or two plants. You may also find gynoecious seeds which are all female and require no pollination. You might also see some labeled monoecious. They, too, are hybrids, but will have both male and female blossoms on the same plant.

There are a lot of cucumber varieties to choose from, including several old standard, open-pollinated ones like Wisconsin SMR. Breeding has gone in different directions in the United States and in Europe. The little pickling cucumbers are mostly American bred. The Europeans have been breeding for non-bitter cukes for some time. On both sides of the Atlantic, breeders have been working on burpless ones. There also are a few oddball things like little round ones, extremely long ones and yellow ones.

Q: Last fall we put a good layer of manure (with quite a bit of wood shavings) on the garden. There are some leaves on top. The leaves and manure have not been tilled in yet. There are also some grass clippings that were tilled in last summer and fall. Should we put on some nitrogen this spring because of the wood shavings? Can you recommend anything else to add to make it a really good garden this year?

A: It sounds as if you are off to a good start, and your plants are all going to thank you. If the wood shavings were bedding mixed with the manure, you probably won't need to add more nitrogen. There should be enough in the manure to take care of the problem. Take a look at the shavings before tilling and see if they are breaking down. If they are, don't worry.

If you can still fish out definite slivers and sawdust, it would be smart to add some slow-release nitrogen this spring. You don't want to give a sudden blast that has all your plants deciding to make only foliage instead of flowers and fruits. Too much nitrogen can do that, just as too little can produce sparse, small leaves.

There's no problem with wood chips, shavings, sawdust or wood in any form when used only on top of the ground as a mulch. It is only when it is tilled in that you need consider whether it may create a nitrogen shortage.

When wood products are mixed with the soil, they keep all the microbes so busy they aren't free to hold hands and dance around with your plant roots. Adding nitrogen contributes to the breakdown of the wood fibers so the good soil bugs can spend their time helping the plants you are trying to grow.

As for making good garden soil, the best thing you can do for it is to add anything organic, and you have definitely done that. You do have to keep doing it, though. It's not a once-in-a-lifetime process. Organic material continues to break down and has to be replaced. Also, the plants grown in the soil take nutrients from it, and you want to replace those. The basic rule is, if it was once alive and now it isn't, it's a good thing to put on your garden.

Q: I have a climbing honeysuckle that is overgrown and its trellis is rotting away. Do I dare prune it enough to put up a new trellis?

Q: I have a clematis of the sort that doesn't die to the ground every year. Can I cut it back without killing it?

A: Yes, in both cases, and no, neither is likely to die. It's a safe rule of thumb with a shrub that you can prune half of it away in any given year and you will not have depleted its leaf supply enough to set it back.

This does not mean that you have to cut all the stems off 50 percent. Climbers, like honeysuckle and clematis, would not be very attractive if you cut the whole plant to the same height. Cut some back by half, leave some full length and cut some to the ground. Just aim for an average of half the plant. When fixing a trellis, you will have to cut some of the stems to the ground, just to get to it. Clematis can be pruned even more drastically than honeysuckle. Native clematis tends to overgrow and make a huge tangle like the ones you can see hanging on roadside fences.

The small-flowered native species are hardy here and can be rejuvenated by cutting everything back to eighteen inches. Two weeks after you trim them back, they will be looking fine again. That's something you can't do to most shrubs.

Q: What does "amend the soil" mean?

A: It means that what you are trying to grow plants in is not the perfect home for their roots. Perhaps it is full of rocks or perhaps it is laced with clay subsoil the contractor heaped up around your foundation just before he left. It may be that plants used up the last nutrients fifty years ago or that you either can't keep enough water on the soil or can't get the puddles to drain. You have to improve matters if you want to grow beautiful flowers or succulent vegetables.

Usually amending the soil means adding organic matter. This improves soil texture, adds nutrients, increases water-holding capacity and provides air spaces that roots need to be healthy. The best soils are about 5 percent organic matter. To grow the healthiest plants, you must continuously add something organic to the soil, because it keeps being used up.

Amending the soil also can mean adding sand to a heavy clay to improve drainage. You can achieve the same thing by adding organic stuff instead of sand. In fact, it takes only half as much, by volume, to achieve the same effect.

The only way of improving sandy or gravelly soils is by adding organic material.

Amending also can mean adding fertilizer in chemical, rather than organic, form. But this provides only nutrients and does nothing to improve the soil texture.

Q: I have seen sacks of mushroom compost for sale. What is it and is it something good to use?

A: It is the medium in which commercial mushroom crops have been grown. After each crop all the medium is removed and replaced. It contains a lot of manure.

It is a perfectly good substance for adding organic material to both outdoor gardens and potting soil. You don't want to plant in pure mushroom compost, but you can mix it with your other soils or add an inch or so on top as a mulch.

It has a pH between six and seven, a good range for most plants. It has about three times as much nitrogen as phosphorus, so it is really good for leafy growth and won't contribute a lot to flowering and fruiting. The reason not to use too much at once is that it contains a lot of soluble salts that leach out slowly with water. The salts are in the category of those where a little is beneficial and too much is deadly.

Q: My Apricot Beauty tulips were gorgeous the first year and the second had made a nice clump. This is the third year and they are just gone. What happened to them?

A: Daffodils go on multiplying their bulbs and if they quit blooming, the cure is to dig the whole clump and replant some, giving the rest away or moving them to a new location. Even in the best of circumstances, tulips don't do that. If you dig up non-blooming tulips, you may find a handful of tiny bulbs and no big ones. It isn't worth it to try to save them. You would have to separate them and put them out into a nursery bed, keeping track of which is where, and it would take up to five years to get big bulbs. Some types, like your Apricot Beauty, will simply disappear.

In wetter areas like the Northeast, gardeners treat tulips as annuals, pulling out the plant and discarding the bulb as soon as it finishes blooming.

In our well-drained soils they do better, but two to five years is a reasonable lifespan to expect.

Tulip cultivars are very different from each other. We have some black ones that are at least ten years old and look just as healthy as the first year they were planted.

Q: Why can't I grow clematis?

A: Are you worrying about a black thumb or black magic?

The most likely problem is that you put it in the wrong place. When the clematis is happy in its home, it requires nothing, but it is fussy about its neighborhood. It does best with morning sun and afternoon shade. It does not do well on the west side of a building and dies on the south side unless it gets a lot of shade. It needs to have its roots cool, so even in its preferred location, mulch the area heavily or plant annual flowers around it to give some shade by the time the days get hot. We don't advise planting perennials for shade.

We once made the mistake of putting a healthy columbine in front of a clematis and every year for three years the columbine got bigger and the clematis got smaller until finally we realized what was happening. It took all summer to kill the columbine, but we finally succeeded and mulched the clematis. The next year the clematis tripled in size.

The type of clematis may have something to do with your lack of success. A couple of the species become semi-woody and will not die to the ground in this area. They are what you grow where you want a big vine to climb on a trellis or cover something ugly. The flowers are pretty but small, and the flowering season is very short. One blooms in early spring and one at the end of summer.

Hybrid clematis, which is what we mostly think of when we consider growing clematis, may be divided into early- and late-flowering. You don't want to grow a late-flowering one. The roots may well be hardy, but they bloom on second-year growth. Here the plant is likely to die to the ground most winters and you won't get any second-year growth.

With any clematis, you must be patient. It will be at least three years before it starts resembling the mental picture you had when you planted it, and it can take seven years to reach its full height.

If you have read in garden magazines about clematis wilt, which kills established vines, don't worry. As far as we know, this is not a disease that has ever reached the Intermountain West.

Q: With spring being so late, when will my plants get around to blooming?

A: In a study done in England, they kept track for ten to fifteen years of what effect weather had on flowering times. They discovered that for spring-flowering plants, it was the weather a month or two earlier that affected how soon they would flower. Those flowering in summer were affected by the weather four months earlier. So if you want to know the answer you must start with the particular plant you are worried about and count back. If it was particularly cold a month or two before you normally expect spring flowers, they probably will be late and if it was extra warm four months before your summer blooms usually pop out, they might be early (and vice versa) no matter what happened in the last few weeks.

Q: When and how often should I fertilize my plants and with what?

A: With the trees, shrubs and perennials, the most common mistake gardeners make is over-fertilizing. It is definitely not a case where more is better, and indeed, too much can cause a lot of problems.

Recent research by nurseries showed that heavy fertilization produces quickly grown plants that are big enough to sell, but they aren't healthy. Those with too much fertilizer are much more susceptible to insect damage of a variety of kinds.

Fertilizer stimulates the top growth on the plants, and too much throws the top and bottom out of balance. You get too much top and at the same time, the extra fertilizer actually slows down the root growth.

Since the plant depends on its roots for a lot of its food, it is not going to be as well fed with a small root system. It doesn't have as good a store of carbohydrates because it doesn't have a place to put them, and it is also shortchanged on a number of defensive chemicals that plants use to protect themselves from bad bugs.

If you are talking about annual flowers or vegetables, they have a short time to grow a lot, so they need soils with a high level of nutrients. Give them fertilizer once a month. But perennials and the whole range of woody plants do best with limited resources. They are pretty good at scrounging their own nutrients and can even get some of their minerals from rainwater. If you give them compost and/or mulch, that well may be all the fertilizer they need. Treat all woody plants like grass, giving them nitrogen and not worrying about the other elements at all. If you give them nitrogen, go easy on it and make it a slow-release form.

We have talked before about the healthiest grass being that with no fertilizer or very little. We have suggested that if you want to fertilize your grass you put just a little on the spots that look sickly. The same rules apply here as with trees – too much fertilizer makes for smaller root systems and, therefore, less healthy grass.

For perennials, annuals and non-leafy vegetables, use fertilizer higher in phosphorus and lower in nitrogen than you would ordinarily use. The middle number on the bag should be larger than the first one.

Here is something from the "It's a Poor Day When You Don't Learn Something Department." Years ago, we found a recipe for soil-less mixes and decided to make our own seed-starting soil. We had very poor luck. Seeds did not come up well and the difficult varieties didn't come up at all.

We went back to buying seed-starting soil and still do. But we just recently learned what the problem was – all the recipes had vermiculite in them. We had a big sack of vermiculite that had spent its previous life as insulation in a building. What we just learned is that when you are using vermiculite in any kind of potting soil, you have to be sure you have what is called "agricultural vermiculite." That used for insulation has been treated with Captan, which is a fungicide. Captan inhibits seed germination.

Q: What is meant by the term cultivar?

A: A cultivar is shorthand for "cultivated variety." It is a particular variety of a species that can be reproduced by cuttings or from seed to have characteristics better than the original species. For instance, let's take *Heuchera* (coral bells). The species *H. americana* is an OK plant with green leaves and white flowers. But if you get the cultivar called "Palace Purple," it has big purple leaves. It makes a very striking foliage plant, as well as a flowering one. That cultivar can be grown from seed and you needn't buy a clone.

The term cultivar gets more confusing when you buy any flower by a name like "Mrs. Jones's Favorite," "Palace Purple," or "Bright Eyes." You might think you are buying a cultivar, when what you actually are buying is a plant with a trademark name. How to tell the difference? What is the difference? If you are looking in a reference book, the name will be a cultivar. In a catalog or magazine, it may be either a cultivar or a trademark.

Until fairly recently, this was not a problem. Then the Bottom Line Factor entered the picture. Someone who develops a cultivar gets a patent good for 17 years. But at the end of that time anybody can grow it and you no longer get a fee for plants sold. If you register a plant under a trademark, you can keep renewing the trademark for all time, as far as we know. Furthermore, you can register your *Heuchera* as "Palace Purple" and then register the same plant all over again under an entirely different trade name – you could call the same plant "Caesar's Robe" or anything else you wanted to, and that would be the trademark. If it turned out it didn't sell well under the name "Caesar's Robe," you could change the trademark to another name – maybe "Emperor." If that isn't confusing enough, you also could pick a purple geranium from your collection and transfer the trademark name to that. This is why it is a little hard to know what's in a name.

Q: What is a cold frame? How do I make a cold frame? What is a hot bed? When is the time to plant vegetables in my cold frame?

A: Think of a cold frame as a greenhouse you can't stand up in or one just tall enough for plants to stand up in. It is a protective place where you can grow plants out of the wind, warmed by the sun more than in the open garden. A cold frame extends your gardening season by letting you plant things earlier in the spring and grow them later into the fall.

It is a frame because it is a box you build and it is cold because it has no source of heat except the sun. A hot bed is a cold frame with heat. The first hot beds were made about 200 years ago in Europe and were heated with fresh horse manure. You dug a big hole, put in fresh manure, and covered it with topsoil; the heat of decomposition in the manure actually warmed the soil. These days hot beds are more often warmed with a weatherproof heating cable buried a few inches in the ground.

As for making a cold frame, there are as many ways as human ingenuity can come up with. The simplest is a rectangle of straw bales with an old storm window on top. If you feel like getting a little more complicated, you can stand four old boards up in a square and stake them down or nail the corners together. You can insulate your frame by inserting rigid foam insulation or any other insulating material that strikes your fancy.

Since your source of heat is the sun, you can angle the top to slant toward the south so it will get more sun than it would if it were parallel with the ground. You can get the angle by cutting the top of the boards at a slant or by putting the frame on a south slope.

The top can be anything that lets in sunlight and heat. For a lighter weight top, you can take the glass out of an old window and replace it with plastic. To get some insulation on the top you can use a layer of glass and one of plastic or two layers of plastic with air space in between. You can buy plastic fabrics especially made for cold frames and greenhouses that don't get brittle from ultraviolet light and that diffuse the sunlight so that even on a hot, bright day the sun won't scorch tender plant leaves.

There is now on the market a lightweight, portable cold frame made all of insulated plastic that you just pick up and carry out to the garden and set down. One advantage is that you can rotate the frame onto new soil, rather than rotating the soil that is inside a fixed frame.

You need to create a system for opening the top of your frame in hot weather. It can be as simple as sliding back the storm window a couple of inches or making a stick with notches to hold the top open at different heights. You also can buy automatic vent controls that raise and lower the top as the temperature inside rises and falls.

Cold frames can be as long as you like, but you never want to have them more than four feet wide because you have to be able to reach all the way across.

Knowing when to start planting will come partly from your own experience. It is really possible to use a well-constructed cold frame year round, but at different times of the year you will be using it for different things. In the winter it is a good place to put young perennials, shrubs or even trees to give them winter weather less severe than it would be outdoors. If you want to plant cool weather plants like lettuce, radishes, spinach and onions, you can start them at least a month ahead of when you could plant them in the open garden. Write down the dates and temperatures, and after a couple of years you will be able to make a good guess.

You can also use the cold frame to harden off flowers you are going to plant outdoors or to start the really warm-weather plants like melons and eggplant, which you can continue to grow in the cold frame all summer long. Late spring is the time of year when, if you have a cold frame, you suddenly wish that you had three.

Q: Some of my foundation plantings look terrible this spring – like dead. Why would they winter kill if they were protected near the house? Was there something about this last winter that caused it?

A: It probably is not winter kill and the problem probably has nothing to do with the past winter.

Foundation plantings don't usually die from winter kill, but from drought. In winters when we have an enormous amount of snow, first it serves as mulch and then it waters the foundation plantings as it melts.

In normal winters, you can have a pretty wide strip around the foundation that gets no water at all. The width of the strip depends on how wide your roof overhang is and which side of the house the bed is on. On the west and north side, some rain and snow will be blown in and the strip will be narrower. On the south and east, the strip will be wider because the prevailing wind blows the moisture away from the house.

What you can do about it is to mulch well and check for soil moisture in the fall. After you think you are through watering everything for the season, check once or twice more around the house to make sure the plantings are going into dormancy with nice, wet soil. How much late watering you will have to do will depend on how many nice sunny fall days there are. Check again early in the spring before you need to water generally; water foundation plantings by hand if they are dry. That will usually take care of the problem, but it's not a bad idea to go out and check in January or February if we get some nice sunny days and the surface temperature gets above freezing. The plantings may need an extra drink then, too.

Q: What can I plant under maple trees?

A: Planting things in containers is a pretty good way to go. The dry shade under a tree is the most difficult type of shade to deal with. Maples are especially bad because they have so many roots near the surface. They compete with other plants for space, and especially for water. Since the tree is so much bigger than anything you plant for a ground cover, it almost always wins.

If you don't want to use containers, there is one very nice perennial that tolerates dry shade and even can succeed under a maple tree if you give it a little extra water. It's called Epimedium and sometimes you will see it referred to as Bishop's Hat because of the shape of the flowers.

However, since it is not well known it can be hard to find. If it is ever grown from seed, we don't know about it, so you have to buy plants to start with. There are several species and you need to check descriptions because not all are hardy here. Epimedium really are very nice shade plants. Although they cannot be grown where you don't have a tree or building to shade them, they really ask nothing else of you. They grow about a foot tall. They are long-lived and are very pretty throughout the growing season. The leaves are mostly heart-shaped and will usually be reddish in the spring while still unfolding and green all summer before turning red-orange again for the fall. They bloom early. The flowers are small, delicate and an unusual shape. We really can't think of anything wrong with epimedium except that it should be better known.

Q: Is it OK to cut the dead, dry stems off my hybrid tea roses? They look ugly.

A: Yes, it is always OK to cut off obviously dead parts of any plant. If the stem is partly green and partly dead, make your cut in the dead part, not the live part.

It is not time yet to do rose pruning that may cut into live canes. For that you need to wait until you hope there won't be any more hard freezes. You notice we say HOPE. The reason you wait is that pruning stimulates growth and if you prune a rose too early you encourage it to grow new leaf buds, which would surely be killed by a hard frost. Wait for late spring; the timing we like to tell people is "when the daffodils are in bloom." Daffodils being hardier than new rose leaves, you should probably wait until the end of the daffodil bloom and not start when the first bud pops open.

Q: Should I prune my lilacs now with the rest of my shrubs?

A: Not if you want to see any flowers. Shrubs that bloom in the first part of the summer, like lilac and flowering almond, made their flower buds the year before. They can't make any new ones this spring, so whatever you cut off is removing part of this year's flower crop, and there is no way to replace it. If your lilac bush looks desperately ugly and you can't bear to look at it one more day, you won't damage the lilac by pruning it now. But if you can wait a bit, why not enjoy the blooms and prune as soon as they are finished? That's the ideal time to prune any shrub that blooms early. You cut off no flower buds and the shrub can get busy growing next year's crop of blooms.

Q: My daffodil clumps look very healthy but there are so few blooms. What's wrong?

A: Do you get tired of us saying, "Well, there are several possible reasons?" Here we go again. We will give you some causes and you can figure out which one or ones fit your result.

If the clumps are really old and have bloomed much better in years past, they may just need dividing. Daffodils like our climate, and as they keep producing bulbs they get crowded underground. A starved bulb can make foliage, but won't flower. If you think that may be your problem, dig the clump, separate the bulbs and replant them about six inches apart.

You may have enough bulbs to landscape your whole place in daffodils and give some to your friends. The cheapest bulbs are the fastest reproducing ones. If you have an elegant pink-cupped variety, you may never have to divide them.

Starvation can come from other causes, too. What is your soil like? If you are gardening on a gravel bar covered with three inches of topsoil, bulbs are not going to thrive. Dig some planting holes ten to twelve inches deep, put some good topsoil in the bottom, then add the bulbs and fill the holes with topsoil.

Is your soil well drained? That is a requirement for the health of any spring bulb, so if your daffodils are at the bottom of a slope, or where they get sub-irrigation, the only cure is to dig a drain ditch or move the bed. Do you cut off that ugly foliage after they bloom? Don't do that any more. Plant some annuals to cover up the drying leaves, but leave them while the bulbs gather nourishment to make new flower buds for next year. The bulb starves if it can't have all the nutrients the leaves provide after the bloom is over.

Do you cut off seed heads that sometimes form? If not, start this year. You want the daffodils to reproduce from bulbs and not from seeds. The energy expended on making seeds should be saved for the bulbs.

And most important of all, did you plant them deep enough? Spring bulbs should always be planted at a depth three times the height of the bulb, which for daffodils is a long way down. If the fall weather was cold and you were in a hurry when you stuck them in, you can try again right after they bloom. The weather will be nicer, even if you are still in a hurry. The standard trowel or bulb planter does not give you a deep enough hole for a daffodil.

OK, there they are – pick from the list. One of those things should give you more flowers next year.

Q: I just bought some plants at a nursery. What do I need to do with them before I set them out?

A: First, turn them upside-down over your hand, remove the pot and see if they are rootbound. If they are, give them a bigger pot while they are waiting to go out.

Introduce them to outdoor Montana gently. Otherwise they might not learn to love the climate and decide to move back to the coast or wherever they were born. Give them a few days of shade, then a few days of morning sun, before they have a full day's sun. Bring them in every night for at least a week. Even if these are hardy plants that eventually will be able to stand cold weather, they aren't used to it now.

Also remember that they usually have been pushed into very fast growth with lots of fertilizer and extra water; wean them gradually to a leaner diet so you don't cause them to sulk and decide they don't want to perform for you.

Q: I bought some rose bushes and am ready to plant them. How do I do that?

A: First of all, since your plants are bare root, stick them in a bucket of water for a few hours. While they are soaking, pick the places to plant them and dig the holes. You want spots that have at least six hours of sun and good air circulation but are sheltered from prevailing wind. If you already know where you want them and it is on the windy side of the house in the shade you will have a couple of hours to think again.

Be sure your holes are big enough to spread the roots well – it's like the rule of thumb for planting a tree – a $50 hole for a $10 plant. Some roses are grafted, and those should be planted so the graft union is three or four inches below the surface. Rose growers in cold climates currently think that deep planting helps to protect the graft from winter extremes; it definitely cuts down the suckering you can get from the rootstock. For roses that are growing on their own roots, plant where ground level was in their containers, not deeper. Do not fertilize at all this year.

Most importantly, those plants have been stored in a refrigerator, so when you get them, they are tender. Plan to harden them up for two weeks after planting. Give them plenty of water; cover them with blankets on any night when it is likely to be cold, and don't give them any direct sun for at least a week. Then for the next week extend the sun exposure gradually.

Q: How should I prune my shrub rose and what do I do about the winter-killed parts?

A: Cut off the winter-killed parts and anything else that is obviously dead now. Then at the beginning of summer see if more has died and cut it off also. Aside from that, you basically prune shrub roses not at all. If there are old rose hips on it now or dead leaves that never fell off, you can take them off. If it is growing lopsided, you can make its outline more shapely. If it is too tall, chop it off – head, neck and shoulders, if necessary.

That is one of the advantages of a shrub rose – it doesn't require the kind of manicuring you give a hybrid tea. You don't even have to cut off the dead blooms. A reblooming rose like a rugosa will bloom again even if you never touch the old dead blossoms, and the dead ones will probably make nice red hips in the fall. If you have noticed that we keep saying nice things about shrub roses, it is because we are smitten with them, especially those that repeat bloom or bloom continuously all summer.

If you have one of the old-fashioned shrub roses, like Austrian Copper, you do need to cut a few of the oldest canes to the ground every year. The best bloom is always on the younger canes. The old ones can get to looking pretty bare and leggy at the bottom if you don't remove some each spring.

Q: Is there any way to fix an ugly old bush besides exterminating it?

If you have some older shrubs and they are all starting to look alike and sort of boring, like a big ball in summer and a tangle of branches in winter, it is possible to prune a bush so it will appear more interesting and more like a small tree. Of course you don't do this where your shrubs are forming a windbreak, because it opens airways at the bottom, but otherwise, it allows you to plant flowers under the bushes.

This kind of pruning can't be done with every kind of shrub there is. The candidate must be a type that produces some stems bigger than others. Alpine currants and small spireas are not candidates – they just put up a crop of small canes every year. But you can do it to any conifer and things like viburnum, barberry, dogwood, lilac, smokebush, and some bushy honeysuckles.

Allow yourself enough time. You can't do this kind of pruning in five minutes per bush. Start out with a picture in your mind of what you want the plant to look like, but don't worry if that picture changes as you go along.

Begin at the bottom. Cut off entire branches at ground level and work your way up. You may think you want just one trunk down there and later decide two or three would be better. Start with the idea that you are going to cut off all the branches on the lower third of the shrub. That may change too, as you uncover one you planned to cut and it has a lovely shape you want to keep, or one you planned to leave that turns out to be really ugly.

Every five minutes or so, you need to climb out from under the bush, back off and take a look at what you have done. Remember that what you do is not going to last forever because the shrub will grow even faster for having been pruned. It is like a bad haircut – if you make a mistake it will be covered up by the end of summer.

Once you see what the structure of the shrub is starting to look like, you enter the second stage – pruning off all dead branches, anything that is obviously weak and spindly and the ones that cross and rub on other branches. When two branches rub together, which one you remove is your choice.

By this time, you should have a shrub that is beginning to assume a very nice shape. It is beginning to look like a miniature tree. Then comes the third stage of pruning, which is thinning what will be the crown of this junior tree. Usually, it is better to thin out a few whole branches and not just shorten all of them.

Take your time in this stage and when in doubt, don't. This stage of the pruning can wait. You may want to finish it as a summer pruning job when the bush is completely leafed out. The work can be done any time before the Fourth of July.

The results are really very rewarding. The most rewarding are the large, overgrown junipers, but be forewarned that you will suffer at least twenty-four hours of juniper rash. We believe you could wear armor plate and still get juniper rash.

Q: I am having trouble with fire blight on some old apple trees. It is worse on one than the others. Someone told me I need to spray with copper sulfate. Is that true?

A: You would probably be wasting your money buying spray. There are two sprays bandied about as being effective against fire blight – copper sulfate and streptomycin. They have very limited usefulness.

The biggest problem is that they would be helpful only if you used them when you didn't know yet that you needed them. They do nothing with existing infections.

There are two cultural techniques you can practice to control fire blight and the most important is pruning. Fire blight is a bacterial infection and the bacterium overwinters in cankers and dead twigs on trees. You need to prune out all the places where it could be overwintering; as the weather warms these spots will start to ooze. That ooze has millions of fire blight organisms in it.

Wherever you prune, be sure you cut back all the way to healthy wood. If you are in doubt, look under the bark where you just cut – red streaks mean the infection is still there and you need to cut further.

To make sure your pruning is helpful and not a means of spreading the disease, you must disinfect your shears after every single cut, using alcohol, Lysol or bleach.

If there are cankers on the main trunk where you can't prune them off, you can scrape around the edges where most of the bacteria will be, but you must scrape down to healthy wood.

If you are careful and thorough, you can get rid of all the active infection on a tree. This doesn't guarantee that your tree won't be reinfected during the next growing season.

Fire blight is most active when the buds first show color but can be spread any time through midsummer. Some trees, as you have noticed, are more susceptible than others, so when you plant new trees, it's important to be sure the variety you choose is fire-blight resistant.

Prune your trees to provide plenty of air circulation in the leafy canopy. Like many plant diseases, fire blight develops best in still air.

The second prong of an attack on the disease is to be sure you don't over-fertilize with nitrogen, which promotes a proliferation of leafy, delicate twigs where the infection is most likely to start. Fertilize only enough to keep the tree healthy – err on the side of caution.

The use of biological controls is offering real promise. Fire blight is most often spread by bees as they pollinate the flowers, but scientists have found two types of beneficial bacteria to fight the disease. One type is similar to the one that causes fire blight. It does not cure the disease but does compete with the bad guys for space on the flowers. The other bacterium actually attacks the fire blight bacterium.

It is interesting that these bacteria are being applied by the very bees that spread the harmful, fire-blight-causing organisms. The bacteria are put on powder, which is placed outside the bee hives. The bees pick it up on their feet, so the researchers are using the cause to carry the cure.

Q: My neighbor told me that I should be brushing my tomato seedlings every day. Is this his idea of a practical joke?

A: We have talked a bit about brushing or otherwise agitating tomato seedlings to make them stockier and more sturdy. It is especially important in this area with our short season because we have to raise our seedlings inside, where they tend to get tall and spindly.

The technique must work because many people in different places are trying variations of the "bang your plant around twenty times when it's tiny" method, and everybody is getting good results. Presumably this substitutes for wind, and it probably illustrates that wind in the right amount and velocity is beneficial rather than detrimental to baby plants.

Three years of trials in Los Angeles used the same techniques on the blossoms of tomatoes of blooming size. The idea is that there might not be enough wind to release all of the pollen on the blossoms, and tomato flowers pollinate themselves inside the flowers. The experimenters vibrated the flowers every other day for one month after they started to bloom. Then they compared them with identical plants that had not been brushed or banged on. The results were universally good with all varieties of tomatoes tested. They got much better yields and significantly larger fruits – really big differences up to 40 percent – and the improvements were found on every plant of every variety.

In 1999 researchers at the University of Georgia tried brushing seedlings of flower plants as well as tomatoes. They used forty strokes twice a day – most testers had used twenty a day. They found that not only were the plants shorter and stockier, but they also suffered less insect damage, especially from the thrips and mites that are often a problem there. The plants evidently were stronger and better able to resist attack.

So, if you come home from work frustrated, bang away gently on all your plants. It's good therapy for all concerned.

Q: I have always hesitated to try growing peppers but want to try it this year. What suggestions have you?

A: When timing peppers, you need to allow about ten weeks from the time you plant the seed until you set them out. In deciding when you may want to put them out, remember they want 75- to 80-degree days and nights that are 60. (Ho, ho, ho!)

They are perfectly happy to have soil temperatures in the 80s. Even if you can't give that to them outdoors, this tells you what you need to do to get them ready to go outdoors.

If you are going to grow peppers, you probably have grown tomatoes. Peppers will take 50 percent longer to come up. You can minimize this time differential by keeping the peppers nice and warm.

Once they are up and growing, don't try to toughen them up. Before you set them out, warm the soil first by covering the pepper-planting area with black plastic for four to seven days. (Clear plastic is better for warming the soil, but it also encourages weed growth under there.) In those few days, harden the plants off, taking them outside to a protected place and covering them at night. If they have any baby peppers on them, take the fruits off at transplant time.

In non-pepper weather – dry, hot and sometimes windy – there are a couple of techniques that seem to help peppers survive. First, you can plant them only six inches apart. Or you can plant two peppers in one hole.

Peppers like to be well fertilized. Different people have developed different fertilizing regimens, but we like to start them off with a complete fertilizer and give them side dressings of nitrogen during the growing season. If your peppers have sun scald, which shows up as brown spots on the fruit, the plant did not grow enough leaves before starting to grow peppers. Try close planting and extra nitrogen early in the season to encourage leaf growth.

If you are a cultivator, be careful around your peppers. They have very shallow roots that are easily chewed up, so don't cultivate under their leaf canopy.

Peppers are so easily stressed by wind that any windbreak you can create will pay dividends. Consider a plastic wall on the windy side or a three-sided plastic enclosure. Be sure that it's roofless.

Put a plastic mulch on your peppers early, then when the weather gets hot, top that with an organic mulch to moderate root temperatures. It also helps to perform all the magic tricks and incantations you can think of. As with most vegetables around here, choose the earliest varieties you can find.

Q: I want to try growing broccoli from seed. Do I need any special equipment or potting mixture?

A: First off, don't do it too soon. It takes broccoli only about five or six weeks to reach the size for setting out. If you live in a very sheltered area you might be able to put the seedlings out in mid-April. The first of May is the usual time. So consider your garden's microclimate, count back five or six weeks and plant then.

You don't need any special containers. We prefer six-packs, but others like sawed-off milk cartons or Styrofoam cups. Just make sure they have drainage.

You don't want to aim for the biggest plants. Try to get very healthy, stocky ones with strong stems and good root systems.

If you plant in six-packs, plant four or five seeds in each little pot. Later you will be thinning to one plant. Start enough to end up with 50 percent more than you plan to set out in the garden. That way you can plant the very best ones. Then give the rest to a neighbor with whom you'd like to compete in gardening. She or he will be grateful and you can walk home with a confident smile on your face.

Barely cover the seed with soil and set the pots in a warm place until the seeds come up. After they are up, the baby broccoli will want maximum light and cool temperatures, but until then only warmth matters. Do not let the soil dry out, but it is important not to allow it to get soggy. Soggy soil issues an open invitation to all manner of fungi and other unsavory interlopers.

When the plants are well up, snip off all but the best one in each pot with a sharp scissors. Don't pull them up or you may uproot the plant you want to save.

It's important to keep the plants growing steadily from the time they sprout. If they have to slow down, at whatever stage, they will not be good plants.

Label every single plant – not just "broccoli," but with the variety. For one thing, every plant in the cabbage family looks pretty much the same when it is small, and you don't want to end up with Brussels sprouts where you thought you had planted your broccoli.

Even though you think you are sure to remember next year what you planted this year, you probably won't, and you are going to wish you know what produced the best broccoli you ever ate. Or maybe you will want to avoid planting the same unsatisfactory variety again. When you plant the seedlings in the garden, plant the little label right there with it.

A week before setting out your broccoli, allow it to get accustomed to the great outdoors, lengthening its time outside gradually.

It is possible to plant broccoli seed directly in the garden. However, the crop will be much later. Also, if plants are well started inside, by the time you put them out they will be too big for flea beetles to kill.

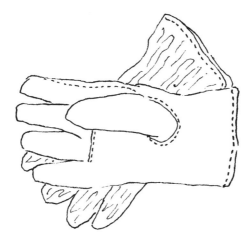

Q: I'm ready to try starting my tomato plants from seed for the first time. I have bought an early variety. Can you help me get started right?

A: Here's a Basic Seed Grower's Manual for Beginners Who Have Never Started Seeds in the House.

Step 1. Buy seed-starting medium. You needn't get the biggest sack, but do spring for the most expensive. Potting soil is OK, but be sure you get the best.

2. Collect plastic containers at least two inches deep. If they don't already have holes in the bottoms, poke at least four. Get enough pots for half again as many plants as you hope to end up with. You will plant the best-looking two-thirds. If some die, you won't be shorted. If they all look great, you can give the extras to friends.

3. Plant four seeds in each container. Set empty pots on plastic meat trays or other saucer-type things. Fill containers to the brim with starting medium. Pat down gently. Make a quarter-inch-deep hole in each container and put four seeds in each depression. If you're feeling brave, put in three. With a finger, smooth soil over seeds so hole disappears and soil is no more than a quarter-inch deep over seeds – less is OK. Do not press down.

4. Run some HOT water (at least an inch deep) in the sink or big,

flat pan. Set the containers in it to soak up water from the bottom. The water needs to be hot so the peat in the soil will take it up – don't worry, you won't cook the seeds. Place the containers in the water two at a time so you can hold them down with your hands. If you don't, they will float, tip over, spill the seeds and clog the drain with potting mixture. Once they sink and settle on the bottom, it's safe to let go and pick up the next two.

5. Leave pots in the water until they soak up as much as they will. They need to have dark patches on the soil surface. Dancing around the kitchen chanting "Hurry up! Soak it up!" doesn't help.

6. While you wait, make stakes – one for each pot. Even if you are sure it is the only kind you are going to plant, label each with the kind of seed and the date it was planted. You can cut half-inch vertical strips from cottage cheese cartons and write on them with crayon or felt-tip marker.

7. Put the labels in the pots and let the water out of the sink. Find clear plastic bags large enough to hold the pots and close the bag securely. You may use a sweater box, a cleaner's bag - something you won't have to open daily to check progress. Insert the trays of pots and close the bag – a spring clothespin works well.

8. Find the warmest place in the house. Light is unimportant, as long as the bags are out of direct sun. Choose a spot where your two-year-old won't pull them off on his head and the cat won't be tempted to play with the plastic.

9. Find something to occupy your mind – it will take at least a week for anything to come up. It is legal to keep checking – look for puddles in the trays or for settling of the potting soil. Think of some excuse – you won't be able to resist looking.

10. Your tomatoes won't all come up on the same day. Not to worry. Your first indication may be a bump on the top of the soil. When the seedling breaks through it will be creamy white and shaped like an upside down U.

The U will straighten up and the seedling will stick straight up. If the seed coat stays attached, it's OK. Two little green leaves develop. If the seed doesn't drop off, the leaves will stay pinched together and that's OK, too. Resist the urge to free the leaves – you'll probably just kill the tomato. As soon as the leaves separate, take the pots out of the bag and move them to your sunniest windowsill. Don't forget the trays, or you will ruin your sill or table. Move each container as soon as the first plant is up. They now need all the light you can provide in the house.

11. The seedlings won't need any water or fertilizer for a day, but

have some garden or houseplant fertilizer handy – lawn fertilizer doesn't count. If you are using houseplant fertilizer, mix at half strength. If using garden fertilizer, sprinkle about twelve grains on each container – it will take time to dissolve and disappear. Follow package instructions when using an organic fertilizer.

12. You may have to water your seedlings each day. It will depend on the weather. You don't want the containers to get really light in weight and you must not allow water to stand in the tray.

13. All that you have to do for a couple of weeks is to watch your tomato plants grow. Normal behavior calls for checking their progress three times a day.

14. When the first true leaves appear (the first pair are seed leaves and don't count), thin the plants to one pot. Clip them off, rather than pulling, to avoid disturbing the roots of the ones you are keeping.

This hurts a little, but perhaps it would help to mutter the mantra, "There is no death – only compost," as you drop the rejects into the bucket with the cucumber peelings and radish tops.

15. If you planted your tomatoes in larger containers than six packs and want to separate them, make sure the soil is damp. Then break the soil into chunks with a plant in each piece. If the whole thing falls apart in your hands, you can still replant the little bare-root tomato if you do it very gently. If you don't need to separate the babies, wait to repot until the tomato is outgrowing its container.

16. If you must touch a tomato plant, hold it by a leaf, not the stem, and under no circumstances touch the roots.

17. Put the plant back into potting soil just as soon as possible. Potting soil is preferable to starting medium at this point in the plants' young lives. Actually, the best mixture would be three-quarters potting soil and one-quarter good garden soil.

18. Put your seedlings into pots one to four inches wide and three to four inches deep. If there are no holes in the bottom, punch at least four – one for every point on the compass. Put a little soil in the pot, set the plant in and fill around it.

19. It is OK to bury tomato stems, as long as the leaves stick out of the soil. Don't forget to move the labels with each plant to its new pot. Return the plants to your sunniest window. Turn the pots every day so the plants don't grow sideways.

20. Start hardening them off a week or two before you plan to put them in the garden. A shock treatment is not what you are after. You want

to introduce them to the real world, but to do it so gradually that they don't realize what's happening.

21. For the first couple of days, keep the babies out of the bright sun. Either see to it that they get only morning sun or drape them with something to cut down on the intensity of the rays – spun-bonded row cover or some other sheer material. Or put them in the shade of a picket fence where they will receive stripes of sun and stripes of shade.

22. Be sure to give the plants plenty of water when you introduce them to the great outdoors. By now they are pretty good-sized plants and will probably drink twice as much as they have been doing.

23. Bring the plants inside at night for the first few days, even if it's not going to get cold. After about three days, you can give them full sun, but they are going to drink even more. If you are going to work in the morning, it is perfectly all right to leave them with their feet in a puddle – they will have drunk it all up by the time you get home.

24. Don't ever put them where the wind can get at them. They will have time for that when they're well anchored.

Q: My uncle in South Dakota grows wonderful tomatoes. He claims he plants them with a little Epsom salts and a little cement. Is he kidding?

A: We don't know your uncle or his sense of humor, but he is probably not kidding. The cement is presumably for lime. In a lot of places, it might be a good idea. One of the places is not here.

Epsom salts contain magnesium. About this, your uncle is not kidding. Magnesium is one of the minor nutrients plants need, especially tomatoes. Several studies have shown that a dose of a dilute solution of Epsom salts sometimes gives a better and earlier yield, but sometimes it has no effect. In any case, it doesn't do any harm.

Q: Can I start my own impatiens plants?

A: If you haven't tried growing from seed the kinds of plants you've always bought in pots, impatiens are a good place to start.

We have grown some lovely impatiens from seed, but have only been able to come up with about two baby plants for each six seeds – not a very good germination rate. We have learned some new information from University of Florida research.

The seed packet tells you not to cover the seed because it needs light to germinate, but the Florida tests showed that as soon as the seed has had enough light to break dormancy, it needs dark.

The recommendation from Florida is that you sow the seed on the surface and place it in bright light at room temperature for one or two days, then cover lightly with damp potting soil and either cover the container completely or place the whole thing in the dark. Check daily and as soon as the seedlings are up, take them back into the light.

Q: I want to start a lot of my flowers from seed this year, but am a little worried about their different requirements. Would you offer some pointers?

A: Your list of sixteen flowers included many annuals, a few perennials and a biennial.

Most of the annuals can be started indoors, but nigella, or love-in-a-mist, and bachelor buttons are tough enough to be seeded directly in the garden any time now.

Godetia and cosmos may be started inside four to six weeks ahead of the time you plan to plant them out, or direct-seeded later, like in May. Godetia doesn't like to have its roots disturbed, so if you start it indoors, put it in six packs, two-inch pots or peat pots and not in a flat to be separated later.

Pansies and petunias take a long time to germinate, so start them early. They have opposite light requirements. Pansies need dark, so cover the seed with soil and the pot with cardboard until the seedlings are up. Petunias need light to germinate, so scatter the dust-like seed on the soil surface and don't cover it at all. Cosmos want a reasonable amount of light, so just barely cover their seed.

The first time we tried cleome from seed we got zero germination, but we tried again the next year. The seed needs light, so cover lightly, if at all. Most important, the pots of seeds need to be put in a cold frame or other protected place outdoors because they require day-night temperature variation.

All the other annuals can be started about six weeks ahead of planting out, although strawflowers can be done a little earlier. The trouble with starting things earlier is that you have to keep potting them up into larger containers until their move to the garden.

Celosia does not like to have its roots disturbed and hates to be chilly. It appreciates being watered with warm water.

Money plant, lunaria, is a biennial that may be direct-seeded any time. It is so tough that it usually reseeds itself. It is best planted behind something else because the pretty part is the seed pods up at the top and the rest can look pretty weedy. Plant your seed two years in a row to ensure some blooming plants each year.

Of the perennials you mention, armeria, or sea pink, and liatris, or gayfeather, are easy to grow and would be good ones to start on if you haven't grown perennials from seed before. Chinese lantern can be very slow to germinate. It's not uncommon for it to take a month. But the plant makes up for its early sloth by spreading, sending runners out to come up where you least expect – and perhaps least want – them.

Perennials in general are quite slow to get started. If you are cramped for seedling space, as most gardeners are in the spring, you can start perennials any time through the end of June. You can keep the young plants in pots outdoors in a protected spot and transplant them to your flowerbed at the end of summer or next spring. By summer's end, they should be in at least four-inch pots.

Growing perennials from seed is exciting. They are not clones and you know only approximately what you will get. Once in a while you will get a plant that is especially large or bushier than normal or has nicer blossoms.

Q: How can one catalog tell you to plant seed one certain way and another say something completely different about the same seed? How can I tell which to believe?

A: You are right – there is a lot of contradictory information. It is very frustrating to us, too. One catalog told us a seed would germinate in two weeks, another said to plant it in the fall and overwinter in a cold frame. A third said the seed had to be cold stratified for two to three months.

One reason it happens is that the person who wrote the stuff down never tried it for himself – just got information from a book – probably written by somebody who hadn't tried it either.

On the other hand, the seeds may be extremely sensitive to soil conditions, so what works for a catalog writer in one area may not hold true for another somewhere else.

In addition, many flowers have erratic germination, unlike radishes, which all come up on the same day, so what you think is affecting germination may not be at all – it may just be the way the seed is behaving. Most flower seeds won't germinate until they have sat around for several months – nature's way of keeping them from coming up in midwinter and getting killed. Most require only time, although some need cold, or even a warm/cold/warm continuum. A few even need to go through the gut of a bird to digest enough of the seed coat to be able to take up water.

Some seeds are only viable for a week or two after maturing and as soon as they dry out, they die. Unfortunately, the profit motive also figures in. Seed stored over the winter and sold the next spring is not going to grow. This is plain misinformation from people who should know better.

The only real solution for this problem of mixed signals is to try some of your seeds each way – direct seed, plant indoors on the surface, plant indoors under soil, cover some with cardboard for darkness, plant some and put the pots in a plastic bag in the refrigerator for a while. Most will be wrong, but something probably will work!

On the subject of flower seeds, delphiniums do well here and are quite easy to grow from seed if you follow a few easy rules.

First, delphinium don't like too-high humidity as babies and will damp off easily if their atmosphere is too wet.

Second, for reasons known only to a delphinium, you do not get as healthy plants if you plant the seed before spring, although the seed still will germinate. You get the best plants if you plant delphinium from seed in April.

And third, don't seed directly in the garden. Baby delphinium plants are the chocolate ice cream of the slug world, and it is highly unlikely you will ever get a glimpse of your crop.

Q: Can I grow my herbs from seed instead of buying plants?

A: You can grow any herb from seed if you can find the seed and if you can get it to germinate.

Herbs are more difficult to start than lettuce, but not as hard as some perennial flowers. Parsley and basil are good ones to tackle first. We have grown oregano, thyme, marjoram, sage, savory, rosemary, chives, coriander, dill and chervil. There are others but this will give you a good start. (You cannot grow French tarragon because it does not set seed and must be grown vegetatively. Just find a friend who has a clump and talk her into letting you take a chunk.)

However, there are some good reasons for buying plants. You might want a rosemary with especially nice flowers or a creeping thyme with blue-gray foliage. These are particular cultivars you will not get from a seed-raised plant. They must be grown from divisions or cuttings.

With the exception of basil, most herbs will germinate best at cool temperatures. Be sure the soil for your herbs drains well and is not too soggy.

Q: Are there some flowers I can grow from seed and not have to buy six packs or flats of annuals?

A: There surely are and quite a lot of them. There are many very desirable annuals you can't even buy in six packs, those that can't be transplanted at all or don't do well when transplanted. With these, you plant the seeds at the end of March or early in April directly in the garden. Some of them will be in bloom before June is over. With most of them, if you leave a few of the seed heads that develop, they will also re-seed themselves, so you needn't start all over every year.

They have the extra advantage of not looking like everybody else's flowerbeds when everybody else is buying their plants at a nursery.

Poppies are among our favorites. There are many kinds, from the peony-flowered ones that grow four feet tall down to the six-inch California poppies. Nigella – love-in-a-mist – comes in blue, white and raspberry, and has beautiful, ferny foliage and seedheads nice for dried arrangements. Clarkia, including godetia or Farewell-to-Spring, was named for Captain William Clark of Lewis and Clark fame. Larkspur, sometimes called annual delphinium, comes in almost every color except yellow and orange. All the centaurea – bachelor's buttons or cornflower – bloom in white, blue, lavender and rose.

Q: I saved seeds from my potted geraniums last summer. How do I plant them?

A: You can plant them, but you may wish you hadn't gone to the trouble. Almost surely, those geraniums were hybrids. Hybrid means that two different geraniums were crossed, using pollen from one type to fertilize another in order to produce a plant with the best qualities of both parents. However, the seeds that plant makes are not going to produce plants like the parent.

The only way to get a hybrid is to go back to the same two parent types and use the pollen of one to fertilize the other. This has to be done every year. Occasionally, after many years of saving seed from a hybrid and saving the seed from only the best offspring, generation after generation, you may get a stable hybrid. This means you can plant its seeds and get plants that look like the parent.

With most plants this never happens. If it does happen, you can be sure it took many years of patient breeding. This would almost surely not be true of the geranium you had on your porch last summer. Let's say your geraniums were a cross between a large, healthy plant with small, dirty pink flowers and a scrawny, sickly plant with huge red flowers, and your plants were large and healthy, with huge red flowers. The seeds from your plants could produce all the combinations of all characteristics of both parents. So you might get some small, sickly plants with small, dirty pink flowers and some healthy plants with large dirty pink flowers and some scrawny healthy plants with small red flowers, etc., etc., etc.

If you think of all the combinations you can get, you see that a seed from a hybrid plant is more likely to produce an undesirable plant than a good one.

If you still want to try, it takes three to four months of good growing conditions to get a plant big enough to set out. You must have a place with a steady minimum temperature of 75 degrees to germinate the seeds, which means you need bottom heat. Geraniums are erratic germinators, so they may come up at different times.

Q: What can I do now to get rid of the weeds in this summer's garden?

A: First you need to change your entire mind set. Approach the problem of weeds not with "How do I kill them?" because killing weeds is an endless process. There always will be other weeds to replace any you kill. Think about it as "How do I prevent so many weeds from growing in my garden?"

Weeds are healthy plants – tough and adaptable. That is what makes them weeds. If they light in a place where you don't care what grows, they are not a problem. They only become pests when they use up the space, water and nutrients that you intended for your tomatoes, petunias or whatever.

If there is a place the truism "Nature abhors a vacuum" applies, it is to bare soil. There is no bare soil in nature anywhere the climate permits anything to grow. In other words, when you till your garden in the spring before planting or when you carefully weed around your favorite spring bulbs, you are really inviting weeds to come in and colonize. You have just created bare soil and immediately the toughest, most available plant is going to start growing there.

How do you cover up that ground? There are a variety of ways.

You can immediately plant something as soon as you expose the bare soil. This keeps the weeds out by increasing the competition for the space.

A second possibility is covering up the soil with something that will shade all the ungerminated weed seeds in it. This is where landscape cloth covered with a decorative mulch of bark or gravel comes in. Even though the weed seeds are still there and alive, they can't germinate down in the dark. You can make a hole in your mulch and plant the trees or shrubs you want. Notice we mention just woody plants. Landscape cloth in a perennial bed becomes a disaster after the first year.

Roofing paper lasts a long time, even in contact with the soil, but doesn't let water through. Neither does plastic. Layers of newspaper last only one season.

Any kind of shading like this is useful under a fence, along a foundation or next to a wall. It doesn't have to be much – a few inches will provide you with a mowing strip. It will save you hours of work with a weed eater or clippers. If what you want next to the foundation or fence is flowers, you are accomplishing the same thing – a few inches where you won't have tall weeds growing between the pickets or among your delphinium.

Consider putting in permanent raised beds for ornamentals as well as vegetables, with paths between the beds. You still will be dealing with weed seeds in the bed, but you will have covered up about half the area where weeds used to grow. It therefore cuts your weeding time in half, and the raised beds will save on chiropractor bills.

You can prevent a lot of weeds by keeping their seeds from getting to the ground. The easiest way is to mulch everything thickly or cover it with plastic at the end of the growing season.

Denying weeds water is another solution. Put in a drip system of the kind that waters only the root zone of your established plants and leaves the area between dry. You are going to have some weeds, but you will reduce the number and kind of weeds and injure the health of the ones that do appear so they won't be able to make as many seeds.

Everyone knows the value of using organic mulch around perennials and shrubs. What you may not have thought of is weeding or tilling one small area at a time and immediately applying the mulch. Most weed seeds germinate very quickly once exposed to light. The record time is thirty minutes, so it is important to cover the bare soil right away.

Grow a variety of plants and mix them. This will help with biological weed control by providing hosts for beneficial fungi and homes for parasites and predators of the weeds.

In any new garden area, think about planting for succession. Plant a tree, surround it with some perennials that will cover the ground sooner than the tree will, then fill up all the area in between the small perennials with annuals. Just cover the bare soil so the weeds don't germinate.

Sell your tiller. Do not till at all. Tilling creates bare soil and turns up weed seeds that have been underground in the dark. If you can't bear this idea, keep the tiller and mulch immediately, one row at a time as you till.

If you are planting a new area or are planning to leave a patch fallow, you can discourage weeds by planting allelopaths – plants that inhibit the growth of other plants. Nothing as complicated as black walnut trees, but try wheat or annual rye, which are toxic to purslane and pigweed.

Allelopaths work in different ways. They give off volatile oils that discourage nearby plants. Rain or irrigation may wash off some of their pathogens, which get into the soil to do their work. The roots of the growing plants may give off some of the chemicals.

Rye is one of the best plants for weed control. If you have a purslane problem where you can't grow rye, you can grow the rye elsewhere, mow it and spread the clippings on the purslane patch as a mulch. Some native grasses, particularly tall fescues and little blue stem, are specialized allelopaths that will inhibit many invading woody seedlings. Be creative. Using a good plant to fight a bad plant is one of the virtues of gardening.

When you are growing vegetables and annual flowers, rotating your crops helps keep weeds to a minimum.

Make every effort to get your weeding done before seeds form. With some weeds, it is smarter to get them out before they can even bloom, because some have the ability to ripen seeds after the parent plant is theoretically dead.

For perennial weeds, you can do a fairly good job of control just by mowing. Mow once with the mower on a high setting, let them re-grow, then mow a second time with the blade set low. Any time you mow a knapweed it starts blooming lower down.

One technique used long ago, which went out of favor and is now coming back, is flaming – burning weeds with a propane torch. There now are special tips to give you a flame just the right shape to do the most efficient job of killing the weeds.

Weed experts say flaming works really well if you use the right technique. You are not trying to burn up the weed, but just to boil it. Move pretty quickly over the area, pausing just long enough that the plant juices boil inside the plant but not long enough to set them afire. If you char them, the plant is more likely to re-grow. You can get pretty efficient at judging that. For just two or three weeds or a few growing in a crack in your patio you can get the same effect by pouring boiling water on them.

If you have an area with so many weeds you just want to give up the fight and start all over, you can solarize the area and let the sun do the cooking for you.

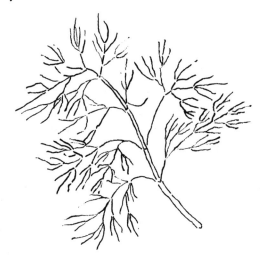

To do a good job, you must get the surface temperature to 140 degrees. Be sure the ground is damp, then cover it with one or two layers of clear plastic and seal the edges with dirt or rocks, creating a flat sauna. Leave it there at least six weeks – in summer, obviously not at this time of year. We suggest that if you take six weeks out of the growing season, you won't have enough time left to grow anything, so you might as well leave the plastic in place until the end of the growing season. Or even to the beginning of the next, which gives you the advantage of keeping out weed seeds that otherwise would have blown in during the cold months.

If you have wondered why your efforts to bring weeds to extinction more often than not have come to naught, consider this: There are an average of between 5,000 and 10,000 weed seeds in the top six inches of one square yard of soil. Some of the seeds are short lived, but enough aren't that after ten years you still will get about 80 percent germination.

If you cultivate after the weeds are up, you will kill about half of the germinated seeds, so by the laws of mathematics, if you wait for them to come up, cultivate every year and no more seeds germinate it will take you seven years to get your crop down to one percent of those original seeds. On top of that, more new seeds than you can take out will blow in, be tracked in, brought in with manure or deposited by birds and animals.

That's why you're not making any headway.

And every time you turn any soil, you turn up more weed seeds, exposing them to the light so they can germinate even if they were buried again some moments later. There are some weeds that need only one minute of sunlight to enable them to germinate. The only cheering fact is that weeds are not immortal. If you do nothing at all, about a quarter of those that germinate will die on their own.

Q: We have several acres with a lot of garden area and landscaping. Someone is building a large house next door close to our lot line. What can we do to keep from being overwhelmed by this big house so close to us?

A: First, let's consider the living fence type screens where you plant fairly near your lot line and it becomes a boundary for your property and a screen for most things on the other side. The problem, of course, is how to get a screen that amounts to anything in the first five years.

There are a couple of different solutions. One is to buy some windbreak fencing, usually green mesh about five feet high, and that becomes the visual barrier for the first few years. You plant on your side of the mesh and when the plants are big enough, take it down. It's not the most beautiful, but it does give you an instant screen.

Another is to plant something very fast growing, but not a particularly desirable plant, because fast-growing ones are not the most beautiful, the most long-lived or the healthiest. You plant them at the proper planting distance and alternate them with a slower growing, lovelier tree or shrub. Then, not more than five years later, cut down all the quick-growing ones. Do not use this method unless you are sure you will cut down the fast growers because they will end up shading and dwarfing all the good ones you planted and they won't have lost any of their bad habits, like brittle limbs that break off.

If you decide to do this, cottonwoods would probably be the best choice for a fast grower, although Siberian elm or boxelder would also be an option. Cottonwoods are not an awfully pretty shape and have a short life span. The elms are brittle and litter a lot and the boxelders attract boxelder bugs.

As for the good trees – how tall do you need your barrier to be? If you need tree height, think about ponderosa pine, juniper or either of two small maples, Amur or Tatarian. The maples both are very lovely trees that are not well enough known. They have no faults except that like most maples they are slow to get established. They mature at about twenty-five feet. The Amur has a more rounded top. You can buy the stock either as a single-trunk tree or a multi-stem shrub. They both are very happy with our climate and soil and will never be weed trees. They have lovely fall color and never get so huge that size becomes a problem. The Tatarian has one additional benefit – the winged seeds that appear in mid-summer start out a bright scarlet color and make the tree appear to be in flower.

These are deciduous trees, however, and if you are worried about a winter screen, you might need a conifer. If you plant ponderosa pines, you may wish to underplant with some kind of shrub or plant a couple of rows of trees in staggered positions so there aren't any big gaps.

If you don't need tree height, there are several shrubs that make good screens and are very pretty. These include lilac, bush-type honeysuckle, redtwig dogwood, serviceberry, shrub roses and golden currant. If you buy shrub roses, get some of the new cultivars that will bloom all summer and not just in June.

So where are you going to plant these things? The tendency when doing any type of border planting is to plant too close to the edge. Remember, especially when planting near your property line, that if anything hangs over into the next yard an unpleasant neighbor may decide to cut that part off some day, and he will be within his rights to do that.

How do you decide how far out is far enough? How high will the hedge be? Will the planting top out at fifteen feet? If so, you plant fifteen feet from the property line. If you expect to shear your hedge and keep it at six feet, plant six feet from the line.

When you first put these baby plants in, it will look like a lot of wasted space, but trust us – it will all get filled up.

One more suggestion for quick screening of the uglies out there – buy the biggest plants you can afford. No matter what size you buy, they will spend a year establishing their root systems, but after that the bigger specimens will take off much faster. This is why big trees cost a lot of money – they have done their growing in the nursery.

But do you really need a hedge? Think of your whole landscape as a painting and use the technique the artist would use – drawing attention to the thing you want the viewer to see. If you look at a painting that has a galloping horse in the foreground, you won't notice whether there is a barbed wire fence on the horizon. In the same way, if you plant one beautiful tree or a group of a tree and a couple of shrubs in the foreground, you won't notice what the neighbors' house looks like. You don't have to cover the whole area.

In order to figure out where to locate the tree, get someone to stand outdoors with a long-handled tool or pole and someone else at a window in the house. Have the person with the tool move to the point where a planting would best block the view of the offending house. Mark the spot and repeat the process from another window. When you have finished checking all the places from which you are likely to be looking at the neighboring house, you will know if you can get by with only one tree and know exactly where you should put it.

Your tree will not have to cover all the outlines of the house. As long as it breaks up the silhouette, that is all you need. This is obviously a time when you should get the biggest tree you can possibly afford.

This is another place we ask you to trust us. If you haven't done this before it is hard to visualize, but once you break up the lines of the house in the next yard, it will recede into the background and no longer appear to loom over you.

Q: My forsythia only had five blooms on it this year, yet I saw some in town completely covered with flowers. What went wrong?

A: Forsythia is iffy around here, especially if you don't live in a nice, sheltered area in town. Otherwise, it might just leaf out and not bloom. It's an early-blooming shrub and stress can affect it any time after mid-summer when the buds are forming for the next year.

It could be that your plant was drought-stricken and the buds dried up and fell off. The first thing a woody plant does under stress is to say, "I'm not going to waste my energy on flowers. I'm going to put it all into staying alive."

The toughest forsythia was developed in Minnesota and can stand cold for long periods. The flower buds of most species, however, are killed or severely damaged by temperatures lower than 10 degrees below zero, even though the wood can live through it.

Q: How do I prune a redtwig dogwood?

A: You prune it like any shrub, which means staying with young growth. You can see that some of the thicker stems are not as bright red. That is simply an indication of age. Cut to the ground some of the thickest stems or the ones with the least color or the ones that are too big for the place you have them planted, which often is a problem with redtwig dogwood.

Ideally, you completely remove one-fifth of the stems every year, so aim for something in that general range. If some stems are too long, clip those tips, too. That is a good way to prune any shrub except the ones you want sheared into a formal hedge.

Q: How do I prune an arctic willow?

A: You can prune it like the redtwig dogwood, but this is a good shrub to shear into a hedge. You can keep it anywhere from one to three feet high and the same thickness. You probably will have to shear it twice a year.

Arctic willow is a very tough plant, so if yours is already hopelessly overgrown and crowding out everything around it, it is perfectly safe to cut the whole thing back to about four inches high and let it re-grow.

Q: Is it true that I should not prune my maple tree now?

A: Early spring is not the best time. You probably wouldn't kill the tree unless it is a very young one, but the problem with both maples and birches is their "positive root pressure." The pruning wounds go on bleeding at this time of year instead of healing over. That is why this is the time of year that in the Northeast and Upper Midwest people are tapping their maple trees for syrup. Incidentally, some people who didn't have maples used to make birch syrup.

The best time to prune both of those trees is in the summer.

We have been telling people for several years that when they make a pruning cut on any tree they should not paint anything over the wound. Our grandfathers probably would say we definitely should paint all pruning cuts. There still is no real agreement on whether or not it is a good idea. We think we are right, of course. The basic reason is that the very air around the cut has bacteria and if you seal the cut you may be sealing in the bacteria, thereby causing an infection in the pruned tree.

Plants are very good at building a wall around any of their own damaged tissues. If you seal the tree's "skin," you actually are slowing down the process by which the tree heals itself.

However, the USDA has been doing some research on tree-trunk wounds caused by machinery such as lawnmowers. They discovered that if you wrap that sort of damage in black plastic it helps the tree close the wound faster than if it were left unwrapped. No research has been done on using black plastic on pruning cuts, but it probably wouldn't hurt to try it if you have a cut in a place where it is possible to wrap it.

Q: I have been preaching recycling and I know I should be composting. How do I get started?

A: All you are doing when you compost is helping vegetable matter rot in one place so you can recycle it back into your garden. Everything that grows in the garden has taken all its nutrients from the soil and you want to put all those goodies back, plus any others you can beg, borrow or steal.

The easiest and most attractive way to do this is to rot all that organic stuff down into a nice, dark brown, good-smelling compost. You can make it as simple as piling up everything that comes out of your garden and yard and anything your friends care to contribute – plants, weeds, grass clippings and leaves. Add all your kitchen garbage except animal products – no meat, bones, grease or dairy products.

There are two good reasons to exclude animal products. First, they attract dogs, cats, skunks and other undesirable visitors to your compost pile. Second, a pile containing animal products will smell bad. If someone told you that you have to put your pile in an out-of-the-way place so the smell won't revolt your neighbors, compost piles he had known must have contained animal stuff. Purely vegetable compost smells earthy, clean and all-around good.

Composting is a fine rehabilitation for your weeds. You just need to be sure not to put in the weeds that have made seed. The seed will survive in the finished product and you will just replant them when you apply the compost to the garden.

If you have plants that have died of a disease you know spreads virulently, don't put those in, but if you don't know what killed the plants, don't worry. You may compost some fungus, but the spores are always around anyway.

Although keeping the compost dry enough is a problem east of the Mississippi and west of the Cascades, here the trouble is keeping it moist enough. It's pretty hard to get a pile too wet around here. It just doesn't rain often enough.

Consider putting your compost pile or bin where it will get sprinkler irrigation sometimes. If it doesn't, check the stuff fairly often – it should be as damp as a wrung-out sponge. Georgianna takes hers a milk jug full of water if it gets dry and Molly fills her kitchen scrap bucket with water before adding it to the pile.

It is a good idea not to add more than six inches of anything without adding a layer of something else. It also is wise to shovel on a layer of dirt now and then to provide microbes. Adding a little of some kind of nitrogen helps speed up the decomposition process. A handful of fertilizer or a shovelful of rotted cow manure would be good.

Some things rot very slowly, like heavy plant stalks, tree and shrub prunings, raspberry canes, etc. They can be hurried up by chipping, but failing that, you can just put them in a slow pile of their own and not expect much of them for a few years.

Even without help, all that vegetable matter is going to break down eventually. Even if you do something wrong or fail to do something right, the worst you can do is slow down the process.

It's pretty slow at best. It will be a year before you get much of any finished compost, but once it gets started, it seems to increase geometrically. In a few years, you'll be getting plenty and the whole rigmarole will have become a comfortable habit. And you can feel very virtuous for having preserved such a great supply of nutrients and having saved considerable space in the landfill.

Summer

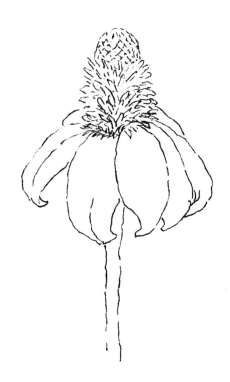

SUMMER

Q: Is it time to tie up the cabbage leaves yet?

A: Cabbages are going to have a couple layers of leaves that lie flat on the ground before they start making the heads. It is not cabbages on which you tie the leaves up over the heads, it's cauliflower. If you have ever looked at an ugly yellow head of cauliflower, the reason for covering the head is obvious. (Not that it hides the ugly yellow, but that the relative darkness keeps the head nice and white.)

Q: I have a peony that is three years old. The leaves on the tips of some of the stems are drying up. It did the same thing last year. I have moved it twice, trying to find a place where it would be happier, but since it has the same problem this year I want to know if this is a bad disease that I can do something about?

A: This is what happens to a peripatetic peony. It's not sick, it's just tired. Of all the plants in your garden, peonies are probably the most conservative. They hate being moved. Yours wants a place with lots of sunshine, rich soil and good drainage. It is going to outlive you unless you are a child prodigy gardener. You shouldn't expect it to have settled in and started to feel really comfortable for at least three years. Lots of peonies are five years in the same place before they feel at home.

Be sure you give it enough water, and even if its spot isn't ideal, you probably would do better to fix the spot rather than move the peony. It would like to have some kind of fertilizer once a year in early spring and if you aren't sure how good the soil is, give it an extra shovel of compost then too. If you believe in talking to your plants, apologize and promise it a long lease.

Q: Somebody was telling me that I could prune my fruit trees in summer instead of winter. Is that true?

A: It is OK to prune in the summer, but it is not a substitute for winter pruning. The purpose of summer pruning is to restrict the growth of the tree. For instance, if you notice a young apple tree has developed two leaders, you can cut one back a ways so it becomes a branch. If your tree is getting really lopsided, you can tip prune the long branches on the side where there are too many. For a limb that is dragging the ground, you can cut it back.

You don't want to do too much summer pruning; remember the old adage that pruning stimulates growth, and in the middle of summer you don't want a fruit tree devoting all its energy to growing new branches. You want it to be developing fruit. Any summer pruning in Montana should be done by August 1. Wherever you prune during the summer, the tree will make new shoots; if it is trying to grow new shoots at the end of summer, they are guaranteed to winter kill because they have had no time to develop any hardiness.

Even if you want to cut back the size of a whole tree, it is best to prune back some of the shoots in the summer and leave some. That way the nutrients will be going into the unpruned shoots instead of trying to develop too many new buds. When you winter prune, you can cut back those unpruned shoots.

Q: Should I cut the leaves off my Brussels sprouts?

A: Well, it's OK, but don't do it just yet. The Brussels sprouts need all the leaves they can grow during the summer to photosynthesize and make the sprouts you plan to eat. Those sprouts will grow like baby cabbages up the stem, one at the base of each leaf. It is handy if you have leaf bases there for them to grow at.

Toward the end of the growing season, if you have a good crop of sprouts, things may get crowded and you may want to cut off the bottom leaves to make more room for the sprouts. At the very end of the growing season, some gardeners think it is helpful to cut off the top tuft that looks like a rose of green leaves, on the theory that the plant will then devote all its energy to the sprouts. We happen to hold a different theory: If you cut off the top tuft of leaves, the plant will devote its energy to growing a new top tuft of leaves.

If you already cut leaves off, don't panic, but let the plant grow some more leaves.

Q: When I put my geraniums outdoors some of the leaves turned red. Was it because I had them too wet?

A: We can't say whether you had them too wet or not, but even if you had, that wouldn't turn the leaves red. It simply is a common reaction to cold air from a plant that has seen nothing below room temperature for many months. If you put it from the house directly into full sun, that can also do it, but sunburn is more likely to make big brown spots on the leaves.

Would you like to know why your plants changed hue? The red color was there all the time, but it was hidden by the green from the chlorophyll. When the plant got stressed out by the cold, the chlorophyll went to the basement. If the plants haven't recovered yet, they should soon and the new leaves probably will be fine. Next year remember that geraniums like to be introduced to the Great Outdoors gradually.

Q: I think the potato bugs were lying in wait for my potatoes to come up. There are swarms of them. What can I do?

A: Stay cool. Bt san diego will come to your rescue. It works on the larvae, which are the creatures that do the damage, not the beetles. You will probably have to apply it once a week until the eggs stop hatching, but it won't be all summer.

Bt *(Bacillus thuringiensis)*san diego is available under several brand names, one of which is Beetle Beater. We know skeptical gardeners who said yes they would try but they knew it wouldn't work, only to announce later that it was like a miracle.

Q: I am growing broccoli for the first time. Last week the plants started growing like mad and now they have flowers on them. What's the part that we eat? Does it come before or after the flowers? What do I do?

A: Quickly cut off the flowers. What you eat are the flower buds while they are still green and not yellow. All is not lost. You can get your plants to make more flower buds this summer. When you cut off the flowers, cut about two inches of stem below them. You may notice that farther down the stem the plant is trying to branch at the base of some of the leaves. Those branches will have more flower buds for you to eat.

Once the buds start to develop they grow very fast and you have to look at your broccoli every day or two so you can pick it at the right time. When the buds are teeny-weeny and tight together, it isn't time yet, but as soon as the individual flower buds start to spread apart from each other, cut them. If they separate completely, you should have cut them the day before. It's not as complicated as it sounds; just cut your broccoli when it looks like the stuff you'd buy at the supermarket.

There are some differences between the kind you grow and the kind you buy. Broccoli for home gardens has more flavor but never gets heads as large as that grown commercially. It does make many small heads after you cut the big central head. When you are ready to pick those on the sides, break off their stems where they join the main stem. The plant won't make another head there, but it will keep making them at the next leaf down the stem until it runs out of leaves.

If you thought the central head was too small or you didn't get a good crop of side heads, be sure to write down the variety you planted this year and plant a different one next year. It may take you a few tries to find the one that does best in your garden.

Q: I bought some Bt to kill cabbage worms but now I am afraid to use it for fear of killing some other caterpillars that would hatch into beautiful butterflies.

A: You have nothing to worry about unless your cabbage plants are all over your flower garden. Just spray the Bt on the cabbage plants where the cabbage worms are eating. You would kill other caterpillars if they were there but they won't be. They will be elsewhere on other plants, flowers or bushes. There is no way for the Bt to get from the cabbage plant to the butterfly caterpillar on some other plant.

Q: For two years my potatoes have had little black lines in them. They look like worm tunnels, but I haven't found any worms. They sometimes go an inch into the potato. What is causing this problem and what do I do about it?

A: Sounds like you have a generous supply of flea beetles. The answer is row covers.

Flea beetles are the little tiny beetles you find in the first part of the season. They are called flea beetles because they are tiny and when you reach for them they jump away. You never get to look at them closely.

Most of the damage they do in vegetable gardens is insignificant, not because they don't try, but because what is a full meal for them won't hurt the plant much. They leave behind tiny little holes in leaves that make the leaves look as if fairies had been using them for target practice with tiny BB guns. That is how the adult beetles do their damage. They can cause a problem if you have seedlings coming up at the time they are the hungriest. Six holes in a three-inch leaf don't do any real damage, but six holes in a seedling's first leaf can kill that baby plant.

Your potato problem comes not from the adults but from the larvae. Most of the time they don't cause any problem, but occasionally with root crops they do. As you thought, the black lines are worm tunnels; it's just that they are made by miniature worms. The worms are not there any more. After dinner, they left, but the potato turned black around the hole, just like a peeled potato does if you leave it out on the counter.

The easiest way to solve the problem is to get some floating row covers – the spun-bonded polyester sheets five or six feet wide. It comes in three or more weights, but for this purpose, the lightest will do. We like row covers a lot because they are good for so many other things. Just lay the row cover over the potato plants and weigh it down. You needn't have a tight seal – the beetles will be coming from above – and leave it on until most of the eggs have been laid. You don't have to go out with your hand lens and hunt for flea beetle eggs. If you don't see the adult beetles jumping around any more, they have moved on to another stage in the flea-beetle year. By the middle of July it is almost surely safe to take off the covers.

We recommend that you do this two years in a row. We would guess that you won't have to do it for the rest of your gardening life.

Q: I've been growing Black Prince tomatoes ever since you mentioned them and I love the flavor and color. But what do I do about the circles on top and the splits?

A: Unfortunately, you can't do much. Cracks are one of the bad things about Black Prince and you just have to decide if the good points outweigh the bad. Cracks on tomatoes come from alternating wet and dry conditions, especially when they are ripening. Some varieties are much more susceptible than others and Black Prince is very susceptible.

There are other physiological problems with tomatoes caused not by disease but by growing conditions. In almost all cases, some varieties will be more prone to them than others. You have to decide if having that particular tomato is worth the problem that goes with it.

One of the most common is blossom end rot. That's the hard brown spot that develops at the end away from the stem. Sometimes it is very small, but sometimes the brown spot gets to a pretty good size with hard, dark flesh underneath it. Blossom end rot is not a rot at all, but is caused by lack of calcium and uneven watering. Blossom end rot is most common in tomatoes grown in containers because it is so hard, in hot weather, to be sure that the soil never dries out.

Blotchy ripening is caused by a period of cloudy, cool weather, followed by hot, sunny weather.

Cat-facing is occasionally caused by a big wind. In tomatoes the most frequent cause is a period of low temperatures three weeks before the blossoms open and it is one of the problems to which some varieties are particularly susceptible.

Green or yellow shoulders come from high temperature and direct sun on the fruit while it is ripening. The green or yellow color is caused because the chlorophyll doesn't break down the way it usually does. It can happen in a lot of kinds of tomatoes, but occurs only in varieties that are missing the gene responsible for uniform ripening.

Sunscald is a brown spot caused by too much sun on the tomato and is usually prevented naturally by the shade the leaves give the fruit. You most often get sunscald on tomatoes you have staked and pruned, and you can avoid it by leaving enough leaves to provide shade as you prune your tomato.

Puffiness is a term for tomatoes that have none of the usual gelatinous material around the seeds. This is the result of poor pollination, which may have been caused by cold temperatures during pollination time, or from too much nitrogen in the soil.

Zippering is the little jagged line running from top to bottom. This comes from low temperatures during the time when the blossom fell off the plant. This, again, is more prevalent in certain varieties.

Q: Your column about rust really hit home with me. My raspberry plants have rust spots and I assumed it was because they are right next to hollyhocks that have rust. My neighbor gave me a fungicide and I sprayed the raspberries. What I need to know now is if it is safe to eat the berries.

Q: Lots of my aspen leaves have black and brown spots. Should I worry? Should I be doing something?

A: You need to check the label on your friend's fungicide container to see if it is safe to use on food plants and if it is, look for how close to harvest it can be used. If it doesn't say the product is safe for food crops, don't eat the berries.

Remember that all rusts are host-specific. A rust attacks one type of plant or a few select types. You can be sure that the rust on your hollyhocks cannot infect your raspberries, no matter how close together they are. The two plants are not related at all. The fact that they both have spots is just coincidence.

Some rusts require two host plants and alternate between them, like the one that needs junipers and apple trees. White pine blister rust uses currant bushes as an alternate host, which is why it is against the law to plant currants in any area where white pine is an important timber crop.

All rusts are parasitic. They get their name from the color of their spores. Each kind of rust can have more than one type of spore and some have as many as five types, including a resting one that sits around all winter and reactivates the next spring.

The spores are carried by the wind from one plant to another. The single-plant rusts like rose rust and hollyhock rust are much more common than the ones that require alternating hosts. There is no connection at all between the rust on roses and those on hollyhocks, except the contribution that weather has made. Rusts, like all fungi, are happier when it is cool and damp than when it is hot and dry.

The best way to deal with rust is to cut off the parts of the plant with rust on them as soon as you notice it. That won't cure the problem, because rust spores are very tiny and can blow a long way. However, you do a lot in your immediate neighborhood by decreasing the spores that are right there handy. You can attack the problem with various fungicides, but don't expect that you will be seeing the end of rust in your garden.

A lot of flowers never get rust, so you can stick to planting those. Even among the most susceptible flowers, like roses and hollyhocks, some varieties are much more resistant to rust than others – plant only the tough types.

The spots on the raspberries probably are not rust. There is a much larger group of fungal diseases than the rusts, which are called leaf-spot diseases. They also are host-specific, so a leaf spot on your raspberries would not be related to a leaf spot on your strawberries.

A few leaf spots can become widespread enough on a plant to cause it some damage, like one that attacks tomatoes in the eastern United States. But basically, leaf spots are only a cosmetic problem. They kill the area of the leaf where the spot is, but the rest of the leaf stays healthy and some leaves on a plant with the disease have no spots at all.

Leaf spots are fairly common on woody plants. If you were to look in late summer at quaking aspen, you would not go very far before you found aspen with leaf spot. Probably no summer goes by without someone asking us what's wrong with their aspen tree and what they should do about it. Their answer is the same as for raspberries – nothing.

Late summer is the time you start noticing leaf spot on a lot of different plants. The conditions are right for the fungal spores to fly. This year's leaves are getting old and not as immune to fungal disease as when they were young. But you don't have to do anything more drastic than just look at the spots for the rest of this growing season. That's a good thing, because these are widespread fungi and no matter how strenuous a measure you take, it probably would not be effective.

There are an awful lot of problems out there in the garden that don't need to be solved. Leaf spots are a good place to practice "scientific neglect." A fungicide spray is not going to cure the spots and doing nothing is not going to make them worse. Never spray until you are sure exactly what you are spraying and why, and you know that it really MUST be done. Otherwise, you are just wasting your time and money on something you don't need and you may well do bad things to the environment. In addition, there are very few pathogens that don't learn after a while how to become immune.

Q: Insecticidal soap is so much more expensive than regular household soaps. Is there really any difference or can I just use dishwashing liquid?

A: Sometimes you hear insecticidal soaps described as fatty acids. Strictly speaking, any soap is a fatty acid. The ones that are commercially produced to do in insects are the potassium salts of selected fatty acids. We don't recommend the dish detergents because they are different fatty acids. They also have degreasers and solvents that are more likely to damage your plants.

Never mix soaps with any other kind of pesticide. Don't spray them on any plant that is under stress – don't use soap sprays on plants in dry soil and don't spray on a really hot day.

One advantage of the insecticidal soaps is that they say on their labels what plants not to use them on. With any kind of soap spray avoid sweet peas, fuchsia, bleeding heart, begonias, gardenias and some ferns.

If you have tried a soap spray and thought it didn't work very well, you might want to check to see if you have hard water. It does not work very well in hard water. If you aren't sure about your water's hardness, mix up some of the spray solution and let it stand for half an hour or so. If there is a scum on top, the water is hard and you need to find another water source for your soap.

Insecticidal soaps are especially good for soft-bodied insects like aphids. They kill by melting the cuticle, the insect equivalent of skin, so they kill some hard-shelled insects, too. They will not hurt any mammal, including you and the neighbor's cat. They break down quickly and completely.

However, you have to put the insecticidal soap on the bug in order to kill it, so you could spray every needle and twig on every fir tree in your garden and it would do no good if the aphids don't arrive until tomorrow. The bugs need to be there and you have to get into all their hiding places. This is why you usually have to spray several times. Probably once a week is good enough for most insects, but for aphids, twice a week is better because while you are filling the sprayer, the next batch is born. Think of it this way: Insecticidal soap is not more expensive if you end up killing even a few plants with the dish soap.

Q: Some of my strawberries look distorted. What could be causing that?

A: We know of two things that can cause funny-shaped strawberries. One is poor pollination. Every strawberry seed must be pollinated in order for the berry around it to develop, so an incompletely pollinated berry can cause the fruit to grow only on one side. The other cause is too vigorous cultivation around the plants. If you distress their roots, you distress the berries, too. You can expect that this problem will go away and you almost surely have no incurable disease.

Q: What is wrong with the plants I have with all these globs of foamy stuff on them? Is it a disease?

A: This is not a disease but a self-applied protective covering of spittlebugs.

They are the immature stage of a soft-bodied insect; they surround themselves with a puff of saliva-like substance to deter predatory insects. Although they do suck a bit of juice from the plant, they really don't do much damage.

They are ugly, we agree, and if they really bother you, hose them off. Even if they find their way up onto other plants, perhaps they will be in a less visible spot.

They will be around feeding for about six weeks, the length of time it takes them to mature. However, they have only one generation a year, so when they are gone, they won't be back 'til next spring.

Q: I have something making a white pattern on some of my spinach leaves. They started several days ago and each day the affected leaves get more lines. What causes this and how can I stop it? Can I eat the spinach that isn't affected?

A: This is caused by leaf miners, a common pest in spinach, although not usually in Montana spinach. You are more likely to find them in your columbine or chrysanthemum than in the vegetable garden.

As bugs go, they are pretty fascinating. The adult is a tiny little fly about 1/12 of an inch long. It has an ovipositor with which it stabs a hole in the leaf surface to lay its egg inside the leaf. Interestingly, before it actually lays the egg, it turns around and tastes the leaf. Apparently it is checking to make sure this leaf provides a suitable place for its baby to grow up. We have never actually watched this phenomenon but are taking the word of entomologists who presumably have documented the behavior. The larva then grows up between the top and bottom layers of the leaf, eating the green stuff and leaving the cuticle, hence the white trail.

When it is ready to become a pupa, it eats its way to the outside and falls down to the ground where it pupates. The larva spends about a week eating and growing and the pupa takes about a week and a half to emerge as a fly. It is less than three weeks from the time the egg is laid to the next mature fly. So even in our short summers, you can have several generations.

It is very hard to spray something that is between the layers of a leaf. Don't bother trying any of the broad-spectrum insecticides because virtually all leaf miners have become immune to all of them. Commercial growers used the pesticides so heavily that leaf miners developed immunity very quickly.

Unless you have an enormous number of them, the easiest thing to do is just pick off the leaves with miners in them and eat the rest of your spinach. If they are only in one end of the leaf, you can eat the other end because if the tunnel isn't there, neither is the bug. If your infestation is REALLY bad, you can cover your spinach with floating row cover as soon as it comes up and grow it under there all season. The flies won't be able to get to the leaves to taste and deposit.

Q: I have already sprayed with everything I can think of to get rid of the aphids and they will be gone for a while, but soon are back. I think they are killing my plum tree – it's not even setting fruit. Is there no solution?

A: Even though they are repulsive and you think you have billions of them and they scare you to death, aphids almost never are a big problem to the plant. The leaves may curl up and look terrible, or you may have a bad infestation on a tree and it rains honeydew. But as for hurting the plants, the damage you see probably has a different cause. The one type of plant aphids really can kill is little baby seedlings – it doesn't take many aphids to suck the life out of a half-inch plant.

The first treatment for aphids is to try to sit on your hands and see what nature will do. This is the most difficult thing in the world to do because they are so visible and so ugly. However, they are at the bottom of the food chain in the insect world and many beneficial insects find them delicious for breakfast, lunch and dinner. They also are a choice item for some of the birds that frequent your garden. Sometimes if you can stand not spraying anything for a week, the problem will take care of itself.

The second thing you try is a fairly hard water spray, which does not kill a lot of aphids, but will knock a lot of them off. Not being the smartest creatures in the universe, it takes them quite a while to get back where they came from – if they ever do.

The third course of action is to look for ants. Ants with aphids are bad news because they herd them as we do domestic animals and collect the honeydew the aphids secrete. They also will attack many beneficial insects that would eat the aphids. You are most likely to notice ants if the aphids are on a tree where you see them marching up and down the trunk. In case of ants, put something like Tanglefoot on the trunk to keep the ant traffic down.

If you really must spray something more potent than water, you have some choices less drastic than the insecticidal atomic weapons. The most selective one is our good friend neem. It is very effective on aphids. As far as anybody knows, neem will not harm beneficial insects, except for honeybees, and it will kill them only if you spray it directly on the bee. If you spray the plant and the bees come later, they are safe.

You also can use insecticidal soap, which won't kill a lot of beneficials, but does kill any soft-bodied insects, good or bad.

Q: I suspect my perennials may need dividing. How do I know which ones need splitting, which can be divided, when and how to do the dividing?

A: Almost all perennials can be divided. The exception is those that have tap roots, like columbine. There's nothing to divide. Either you have the root or you haven't. There usually are techniques for splitting up a perennial by root or stem cuttings if you have to multiply it, but it is not easy. There are a few that absolutely hate to have their roots disturbed.

You can tell if a perennial is going to be easy to divide by inspecting the crown any time during the growing season. If you can see multiple crowns – several clusters of stems coming from different points – it is going to be very easy. And fortunately, that is how most perennials grow. One way you can tell that a perennial needs dividing is that the crowns have formed a "doughnut." The original crown has grown old and died but it had already made younger crowns in a circle around itself. This gives you a healthy circle around an empty place.

Other perennials, like daylilies, you can tell need division when the root mass gets so dense it starts choking itself out. If a perennial starts blooming less and there is no other reason, like a late freeze or the dog burying a bone in the middle of it, it probably is in need of splitting. If it is too big for the spot it is in, dividing it leaves you with a smaller plant and another to put somewhere else. If some of your friends are looking longingly at your perennials and you are feeling warm-hearted and generous, you can give away portions of a mature plant without hurting the "mother."

As for when to divide, the absolutely best time is early in the spring as the plant is just beginning to break dormancy. Then the plant has the whole season to get itself re-established. The exception to that is those plants you first plant in the fall so they get their roots established before the ground freezes – like peonies. Oriental poppies, for most of the year, will die when you try to divide them but are perfectly happy to be divided if you do it during their summer dormant period.

We were told years ago by a very good gardener that you could divide perennials any time during the growing season. We have found that to be true. The secret is to make the transition as fast as possible. Have the new hole – or holes – ready before you disturb the established plant. You do the actual dividing by cutting into the crown. Some plants have crowns fibrous enough that you can cut a wedge out with a knife. Some require a shovel and others, like daylilies, may take most of the tools you own.

Dig down with the shovel to get as many of the roots attached to that part of the crown as you can, lift it and move it to its new home as quickly as possible. Never lift the whole plant out of the ground unless you intend to move the entire plant. All you will be doing is severing more roots than you need to. Try to take at least two crowns from the mother plant, just in case one doesn't do well.

If the old plant does have a dead center, you might want to cut that part out and put it on the compost pile while you are in there messing around. Remember to give the divisions extra water for a couple of weeks while they are growing new roots.

Since we are madly in love with floating row cover, we like to use some of the smaller, half-rotten pieces of old ones to cover the new transplants for a week or so. It helps decrease transplant shock.

ROSES – Every year, rose growers come up with questions about rose diseases and pests, and this is an opportune time to talk about them to give you a head start on problems as your rose bushes start the new season.

Diseases are basically fungal and there are three main ones – powdery mildew, rust and black spot. If you are going to combat them, it helps to know something about the diseases so you don't start firing wildly in all directions.

Powdery mildew is the most common disease here. It is happiest when temperatures are about 60 at night and 80 in the daytime. It likes humidity between 40 and 70 percent. If you know that, you know when it is time to start looking for the first symptoms.

It spreads faster when there is dew or fog, but although those damp conditions spread the spores around, the spores won't grow when the leaves are wet – they must be dry. When you notice powdery mildew it is at least two days after the plant was infected. That's how long it takes for the fungus to take hold.

You see it first as blisters that make the leaves curl and then as a gray coating on the leaves and buds, making them look as if they have been dusted with dirty talcum powder. Powdery mildew is very selective, affecting almost entirely the tender new growth. It overwinters in places where you can't get at it – inside the tiny little leaf buds on the canes.

Rust shows up as orange or yellow spots early in the summer and most often on the back of young leaves. It can start earlier than powdery mildew because it prefers temperatures in the 64-70 ranges, a narrower spread, but with a little cooler daytimes. Rust spores require moisture for at least two hours. Given the right conditions it starts a new cycle every ten to fourteen days all through the growing season. Here it usually doesn't last that long because as our summer progresses it doesn't get the required two hours of moisture. It overwinters as spores on old foliage or inside the canes.

Black spot is the least common rose fungus here, being more of a problem in the eastern portion of the country. It does get here on roses that have come in from either the East or West Coast. It likes rainy weather and requires at least seven hours of moisture for the spores to grow. It likes temperatures about 64-75. Once the rose is infected it takes three to ten days for the disease to show up, and it reproduces every three weeks. As with rust, we are likely to see it only at the beginning or end of the season because the middle of the summer has weather it can't abide.

Black spot fungus likes the young leaves, and if you don't have a bad case you will just see little black flecks on the leaves. If you get a really bad infestation, the rose will lose all its leaves over a period of about a month. The spores overwinter in the dead leaves or inside the canes.

What to do? Start looking for symptoms when the temperature first gets to 60. The smartest thing to do is to plant only disease-resistant roses. Rugosas, for instance, have great resistance to most diseases. Hybrid teas are very susceptible to disease, although some are less vulnerable than others are. Grow your plants to be as healthy and happy as possible.

Roses like a fertile clay soil, so if your soil is sandy, fertilize them fairly often. Do not use high-nitrogen fertilizer because that encourages the tender green growth most appetizing to all the fungi. Compost, manure and slow-release fertilizers are the best choice. Plant the roses where they will dry out fairly early in the morning or after a rain. Prune them so the plants are open to allow good air circulation. If you irrigate by sprinkling, do it early enough that the leaves can dry thoroughly by nightfall.

With powdery mildew it is a very good idea, once you see any of it, to go out every day early in the afternoon and hose the plant with water, concentrating on the backs of the leaves. That's the time of day most of the spores are flying. If mildew spores get wet within six hours of landing on the leaves, most of them will be unable to infect the plant. Also, quite a few will get washed right back off the leaves with your spray. Once you start water-spraying them, do it every three days for a month.

For any of the three diseases, take up all fallen leaves that might be infected. If you had a bad infection last year, prune the canes to a height of four to six inches above the graft at the beginning of the season. For powdery mildew, don't prune too heavily during the growing season, because hard pruning will produce new spurts of tender green growth.

A winter mulch is an excellent idea because it makes a physical barrier between the spores on the ground and the plant. Once any of the diseases has appeared you will want to use a fungicide. The commercial ones really only work as preventives and do not control the infestation once it is visible. You also can try baking soda, useful to prevent and to cure the disease. Mix a one-percent solution – two tablespoons of soda to a gallon of water. Some gardeners prefer to add to that two to three T. of horticultural oil. If you decide to do that, don't apply the mixture when the temperature is high and be sure the sun won't hit the sprayed foliage before it has a chance to dry. You also can use neem – a neem oil extract designed for fighting off fungus.

Q: My tomato plants have a lot of green tomatoes, but also a lot of lush growth and flowers. I'm wondering if I should cut off some of that foliage to hurry up the ripening of the tomatoes?

A: No. If you do, you won't have any tomatoes to ripen because it takes leaves to produce the carbohydrates that go to the tomatoes. We don't know if anyone has worked out the ideal number of leaves per tomato (don't laugh – they've done it for apples – it's forty leaves per apple) but you really should leave all the leaves on.

You can cut off the blossoms, however, before they can set fruit. Flowers that come in August have a very poor chance of developing into tomatoes before the whole plant is knocked down by frost.

Also, you can cut off new growth if you have indeterminate varieties of tomatoes. Determinate tomatoes have smaller plants that set fruit pretty much all at the same time. A determinate plant will probably have stopped blooming by late summer and there's not much you can do to hurry it.

An indeterminate plant would go on growing forever, if the weather would let it. If you look at the base of the leaves, you will see where new shoots are growing. In August, those are just like the blossoms. They won't have time now to do anything useful for that tomato plant anyway, so just tweak them off.

This is not a once-over-lightly operation. That plant is not about to be foiled by one pruning. From now until frost, it will go right on trying to make more shoots and more flowers. Pretty soon you find yourself in a battle of wits with a tomato! You probably need to plan on trimming it once a week until frost. In that way you really do force the plant to put its nutrients into the existing tomatoes.

Q: My lettuce is getting brown tips on the leaves. What's wrong with it? Does it have a disease?

A: This is called tip burn in lettuce and in other plants sometimes it is called leaf scorch. It comes from having a plant with a root system too small to keep up with its leaf surfaces when under stress. In lettuce, there really is no way to stop it. When you suddenly have hot sun on all that delicious leaf surface, even when you have a healthy root system, the roots just can't keep up with the drying effect. The part of the plant that is affected is the far end of the water transport system. And the stressed root system just can't pump the moisture that far.

If you grow different kinds of lettuce, you will notice that some kinds get tip burn and others don't. That is really the only solution to the problem - grow the ones that don't. One example is the old standard Black Seeded Simpson lettuce, which is still a very good lettuce but in hot weather is subject to tip burn. There is a fairly new variation called Simpson Elite, which does not grow as fast in cool weather, but doesn't get tip burn in hot weather, either.

In plants other than lettuce, you can get burnt leaves from soil compaction, transplant shock, over-fertilizing, drought stress, or from anything that slows down the growth or injures a root system. If you have leaf scorch in plants other than lettuce, look for whatever might be causing a problem for the roots.

Q: I recently bought a place where the garden is overgrown and difficult to care for. I would like to relocate some of the flowers, mainly roses, daffodils, iris, lupine and peonies. Should I dig them up and transplant them this fall or should I dig them up and let the roots dry before placing them in their new location? I read your column about peonies, but mine are older plants and bloom well. Should I separate them?

A: We have to give you separate answers for when to move things, but first of all DO NOT let the roots dry out! It would be fatal to everything but the daffodils and iris.

If you can still find the daffodils, move them now. If you can't because the foliage is dried up and gone, wait until next spring and move them immediately after they bloom. They will survive that well, as long as you get them back into the ground right away. When you dig the bulbs, you probably will find a lot of small ones. Unless you want to increase the numbers drastically, put the little ones in the compost pile and move only the big ones.

This is the ideal time to move the iris.

The lupine may or may not survive being moved. They don't transplant very well. But they also don't live very long, so if they die, don't blame yourself — just assume it was their last year of life anyway.

With roses, it depends on the size of the plants. If they aren't too big, just dig up a big enough chunk of earth that you get all the roots possible. That can be done now.

If they are very big bushes, you are going to lose a lot of roots trying to move them. The smartest thing is to root prune them now. Make a circle about a foot out from the center of the plant and dig straight down a full shovel-depth. But don't dig under the bush and don't move the plant. You will have cut off a lot of roots, and the bush will respond by growing more feeder roots within your circle. Repeat the procedure in about a month, cutting down into the same trench. In fall, whenever the weather has become cool and rainy, move the bush.

Peonies should be moved even later — the end of September or October. If you want to make more plants, you can cut chunks out of the root mass of the overgrown ones at the same time. Be sure that every piece you cut off the root has at least two buds on it — those little pink button things. If there is one secret to moving any perennial or any woody plant, it is to get it back into the ground as fast as you can after you have dug it up. If possible, dig its new hole first and then take it out of the ground. Roots exposed to air begin to die in five minutes.

The second most important thing is to water the plants well after moving them. We often use a half-strength liquid fertilizer of the kind you might put on your houseplants, to help avert transplant shock. After that, water once a day for one week and every other day for another week.

The reason for the extra water is that you will have cut off quite a few roots and the ones remaining need to have enough water to supply the leaves. It will take at least two weeks for them to grow a significant number of new roots.

Q: I have a tree with so many aphids that the aphids – and some of the leaves – are falling off on the ground. What should I do?

A: Occasionally you get enough aphids on one tree in a bad aphid year that a tree will lose a lot of its leaves, but the leaf-growing season is much longer than the aphid-growing season. The tree will just produce new leaves to make up for those it lost. The worst that will happen is that the tree will grow a little more slowly this year. So fifty years from now, if you were counting the growth rings in that tree, you might find a narrower growth ring for this year. It is improbable that the tree would have that kind of attack two years in a row and even if it did, it almost surely would survive it. Aphids can kill a two-inch seedling, but they are no match for a tree.

Q: Am I supposed to be fertilizing my annual flowers and vegetables? I keep hearing about not over-fertilizing.

A: Annual flowers have one season to grow, bloom, make seeds and ripen the seeds, their only way of reproducing themselves. This is a lot of work for a plant to do in the short season we have here – maybe three months at most.

If you once starve an annual, it will never recover and never be the plant that genetically it was capable of being. This is one reason why, when buying annuals in containers, you don't want ones that are overgrown and root-bound; they won't get to be as big and beautiful as if this had not happened.

The rule of thumb for fertilizing annuals is to feed them once a month. If you put them into good enough soil, they won't need any extra fertilizer for a while, but even very good soil is not likely to produce good growth all season long without some sort of fertilizer. Whether you are talking about compost, manure, organic fertilizers, or pelleted inorganic fertilizers is up to your style of gardening, but do give them something.

Some people will say – "look at nasturtiums – if you give them good soil or extra fertilizer they won't bloom – they just make leaves." That's not really true. Nasturtiums and a few other plants like bachelor buttons can tolerate worse soils than other annuals, but will do better in good soil. When you get annuals that are all leaves and a few blooms, or blooms hidden down in the foliage, it's not too much fertilizer, but too much nitrogen fertilizer. Use a balanced fertilizer with phosphorus in it.

If you want to keep annuals blooming over a long period, it is necessary to deadhead – cut off the faded blossoms. This prevents the plant from going into the seed-producing mode and keeps it making flowers for you. Fertilization makes a difference there, too, because almost all annuals will quit blooming if they aren't fed enough.

Q: My flowering almond was getting too big, so last year I asked the guy who trimmed my hedge to trim that, too. He sheared it back to the size I wanted, but this year it is just huge! It is out of proportion to everything else in my yard. It has a zillion new canes and they grew terribly long. What on earth can I do? Must I keep cutting it back every year?

A: It is indeed possible to shear it like a hedge, but you can see what happens – you get a lot of vigorous new shoots. So you have to shear it often – definitely once a year and probably twice will be better. Remember, you prune spring-flowering shrubs after they finish blooming.

The trick to shearing it like a hedge is to cut it back smaller than you want it to be so it will spend 10 percent of its time being smaller than you want, 50 percent about the right size and the rest of the time being bigger than you want. This sort of shearing will give you a fairly formal look – you can trim it into a ball or a topiary chicken, if you want to. People do, you know. The mere thought gives us a whole new meaning for the phrase, "Not In My Back Yard!"

For a less formal look, the best thing to do is cut out about half the branches all the way to the ground, picking the thickest, most vigorous ones to get rid of, not to save. The plant will be perfectly happy to lose all the big stuff. Also, because flowering almond blooms best on newer wood, this method will make it more beautiful when it flowers next spring.

You will have to do something to your shrub every year. You won't have to take out half the stems each year, but some reasonable number. If you cut many branches to the ground, some of the bush's energy will go to making new ones and those remaining won't get as long. If it is still too big, the only solution is to take it out and plant something smaller.

Q: Somebody gave me a Russian olive and told me it was used for a hedge. Can I put it near the house and keep it trimmed to three feet?

A: Unfortunately, your generous friend had a different sort of hedge in mind. Russian olive can be a hedge, but hedge as in "windbreak." It is a small tree that tops out at about twenty feet. Nothing in the world will make a twenty-foot tree into a three-foot bush. When you try to make that drastic a change in the natural size of something, you end up with either ugly or dead. Unless you are into bonsai, in which case it might turn out only semi-ugly.

A Russian olive is a very tough tree, hardy to Zone 2, which is pretty darn hardy. It is used often for windbreaks and shelter belts on the Great Plains because it will tolerate almost everything, especially drought. In fact, one of the few situations it cannot handle is a lot of irrigation. It is not a bad small tree, an interesting shape. It is not really an olive, but does have a small fruit that looks like a junior size olive.

The tree also is going to be thorny, so you won't want it next to the swing set.

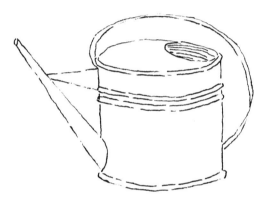

Q: Have you ever heard of a plant called dame's rocket? Somebody has offered to give me some and I wonder if it is a wildflower?

A: Yes, it is fairly common. Also called sweet rocket, damask violet and dame's violet, its botanical name is *Hesperis matronalis*. Once upon a time it was a wildflower, but not in this country. The references don't all agree on its origin. Some say it was native to central and southern Asia. One says it comes from Europe and another says it grew from eastern Europe through Siberia. So we are safe in saying it comes from somewhere in the Eastern hemisphere, south of the arctic and north of the tropics.

Another disagreement is whether dame's rocket is a biennial, a short-lived perennial or not a true perennial. One source says the plants die as soon as they flower. One point of agreement is that they do self-sow, but usually not enough to make them a terrible nuisance – you might just want to thin the seedlings. It is very tough. Even here, you may see clumps of it blooming in places where it doesn't get much water, which is rare for a non-native flower.

The flower is purplish rose and looks like phlox, with four petals on a multi-flower spike. It is not phlox, though. It actually belongs to the crucifers – broccoli, cabbage, etc. If you accidentally let a broccoli head bloom, you will see that its blossoms, though yellow, resemble the dame's rocket.

The flowers are fragrant, especially in the evening. There also is a white form, which is supposed to be especially nice at twilight.

Q: Is it true that marigolds are good to plant in vegetable gardens because they keep down insects and diseases?

A: No and yes. They are certainly not an all-purpose cure for bad bugs and disease. There may be some qualities of marigolds that keep some destructive insects away, but scientific proof is lacking. Somebody says, "I planted marigolds next to my green beans and they didn't get sick that year." Maybe the marigolds had some effect and maybe they didn't. As far as we know, nobody has done experiments using two patches of green beans, one with marigolds and one without, and come up with evidence that one plot got sick and the other didn't.

One case in which marigolds definitely are good at protecting plants is with parasitic nematodes: tiny, worm-like things that live in the soil and feed on plant roots. One of the worst kinds is the root-knot nematode.

A parasitic nematode can be a terrible problem for a lot of kinds of flowers and bulbs, as well as vegetables. French marigolds – the small kinds – are a wonderful cure for nematode problems. Horticulturists have studied this and what they think happens is that the nematodes are particularly attracted to the marigolds and start eating on their roots; then the roots give off a toxin which does the nematodes in, so they don't go next door to eat the cabbages because they started with marigolds and didn't live that long.

The only problem with this happy ending to our fairy tale is that in Montana there are no root-knot nematodes.

Q: How deep do I plant my asparagus crowns?

A: Research from Ontario, Canada, (we assume it would apply here, too) showed they got the most production per acre in commercial growing if they did not plant their asparagus crowns in the traditional way. The old way called for planting them deep, hilling them up and spacing rows far apart.

The Canadian scientists observed the experimental plots over a period of nine years. The beds were planted at depths varying between six and twelve inches. They put the plants ten inches apart rather than the usual eighteen to twenty-four inches and varied the spacing between rows from two feet to four feet.

Then they kept track of the amount produced.

After nine years, they had seven years of harvest because you have to wait until the third year to start cutting asparagus. The best production came from the shallowest plants in the rows with the closest spacing. But the most interesting finding was that when they checked all the crowns at the end of nine years, they discovered they all had moved themselves up so they were between four and five inches deep. The researchers were really surprised – this is completely contrary to common belief about what asparagus likes. Apparently the asparagus just took matters into its own hands – or crowns. We will be glad to check the depth of our crowns and report how deep they are, but not until the season is over. We don't want to accidentally murder a spear. If we were starting a bed now, we would just plant the crowns four to five inches deep.

Q: I have had problems with something tunneling through my radishes and other root vegetables, especially turnips. I'm about to give up even planting them any more if I can't find a solution. Do they winter over in the soil?

A: If the tunnels are already there, it is too late for this year. If not, there may still be time. In any case, you can keep them out of next year's crops.

The worms are root maggots. They mature into a very small fly – much smaller than a housefly. The fly lays its eggs at ground level next to the stem; they hatch, crawl down and feast on your root vegetables.

Insecticide sprays do not work very well. It is hard to get them in the right place and even harder to know the right time to spray. Physical controls are better.

One old standard method is to put something around the stem of any plant that a root maggot can eat where the stem enters the ground – a strip of aluminum foil or little squares of roofing paper. The fly can't crawl down the stem to lay its eggs. The easiest, very excellent method is a high-tech one, floating row covers. If you buy the standard, medium weight cover, it is a good idea to prop it up with hoops of plastic pipe or something to hold it above the foliage. If you get the newer, ultra-light-weight material, sometimes called summer weight, you can lay it directly on the plants. Hold the edges of the cover down with rocks or boards or fistfuls of dirt or homemade wire staples about six inches long. The cover needn't be airtight, as long as it is close to the ground. The flies seem uninterested in crawling under and we surmise that they just go someplace else where they can fly in.

This is a method of insect control that we can recommend as not only good, but perfect – if you put row covers on before the flies start laying eggs. It is smartest to cover at planting time because there are different kinds of root maggots which operate at different times. Err, if you must, on the side of being too early. You will not hurt the growth of those plants at all. A plant that grows under a row cover all season will, if anything, have a more lush top because it has had some protection from extremes of weather. Rain goes right through the material, so even if you irrigate with overhead sprinklers, there's no problem keeping plants moist. We would never grow radishes without it again.

Q: I have some large brown patches in my grass that keep getting larger and browner. Could they be caused by the heavy-duty drain opener I used, going through the drain field under the lawn?

A: That's a possibility, we suppose; however, drought would be our first guess.

To find out if lack of moisture is the problem, dig straight down in the brown spot with a trowel and see how far down the soil is damp. It should be moist down as deep as your trowel blade will go.

If you find there is only an inch or so of damp soil, you might say, "But I just watered there yesterday." To which we answer, as we have many times before, "But not enough." It is much more important to water deeply than often.

If you determine that the brown grass is caused by lack of water, be prepared to give it good long drinks. It is easy to keep moist soil moist, but almost impossible to re-wet soil that has dried out thoroughly.

Is the browning area on a south-facing slope? Maybe that area gets more direct sun. Could the soil type be different in those areas than where the grass is still nice and green? Does your lawn have a high percentage of bluegrass in it? That's not very drought-tolerant.

A special problem with water deprivation is that it takes a long time for the damage to become obvious (and a long time to correct it). The damage was done a couple of weeks ago and it will take you at least that long to see any major improvement, even if you do give it hefty showers.

If the problem were a disease, it is unlikely that it would be in a few large patches – diseases usually appear in many smaller patches that have definite outlines.

It might be that grubs are the culprits. Try grabbing a handful of the drying grass and pulling up, like lifting a toupee off someone's head.

Q: If you don't have to worry about squash and cucumbers cross-pollinating and making strange-looking vegetables, why is it that you have to separate regular sweet corn from super-sweet to keep them from cross-pollinating?

A: You don't have to worry about squash and cucumbers because you don't care what kind of seeds they make. Even if you let them cross-pollinate, this year's vegetables would be normal. But if you saved the seeds from those veggies and planted them next year, that's when you could get the funny-looking – and tasting – things.

With corn, it is this year's seed crop you eat off the cob with butter and salt. If you allow regular and super-sweet varieties to cross-pollinate, the super-sweet corn will not taste like sweet corn – it will taste like field corn.

Q: My zucchini plants made some little tiny squashes, but when I left them on the vines to grow bigger, they rotted. What's wrong and what should I do? I thought ANYBODY could grow zucchini.

A: Not to worry. It has nothing to do with how green your thumbs are. You can blame it either on the weather or on the lack of bees.

This is not uncommon, especially early in the season. It means that no bee got there to pollinate those first blossoms. If you look at your squash flowers, you will see that some of them have the little bitty squashes already there at the base and some don't. The female flowers do and the males do not.

The squash you eat is actually the flower's ovary, which after fertilization takes place, develops into a fruit to protect the seeds growing inside. If the weather isn't good enough for the bees to get airborne for a few days, there are going to be blossoms that don't get pollinated. Therefore, they don't make squash because they don't have any seeds to protect.

Don't worry. Almost surely your later zucchini blossoms will be pollinated and do fine.

Q: Recently my wife read an article regarding raised concrete garden beds leaching something out of the soil, but when she tried to find it to show me, we couldn't find it. I had built a twenty-by-five-feet-by-eighteen-inch bed for my strawberries to make care for them easier. I'd like to know more about the problem and a possible solution.

A: We don't know where your wife read it either, but the problem is not that the concrete leaches something out of the soil, it is that something leaches in. What happens is that new concrete will raise the pH of the soil next to it. By the time it is old, it doesn't happen any more. That's why you can have problems with plants planted near a new house foundation.

By no means is there always a problem. We suggest you wait and see if you are having one. If the plants nearest the concrete start to look chlorotic – leaves turn yellow with green veins – that means the pH is too high for them to be able to absorb the iron from the soil. In that case, you need to lower the pH. If there is no sign of chlorosis, you can assume you have no problem.

There are various ways to lower pH. Probably the easiest is to sprinkle the soil surface with agricultural sulphur and water it in. The best way to get the sulphur is to find a friend who already has some. They will be happy to share, because it comes in very large bags and if they bought it once, they have a lifetime supply.

Q: Disgusting earwigs are driving me batty. Is there something I can do to get rid of them without destroying my beneficial insects in the process?

A: If you can stand it, the best thing to do is nothing. Even if earwigs are repulsive, they are one of the guys in the white hats. They eat spider mites, aphids and other definitely destructive insects in the garden. They do very little damage to your plants.

If you can't stand them, you can roll up and fasten a newspaper and lay it on the ground to make an earwig trap. They like dark, tight quarters, so they will crawl into the folds of the newspaper; you can relocate them by shaking out the paper somewhere away from your garden.

Supposedly a good way to kill earwigs is to set tuna cans around the garden and pour in about half an inch of vegetable oil. We have not tried this.

We agree there are a lot of things in the world we would rather look at than an earwig. But we just steel ourselves, say "Go eat an aphid," and turn our backs.

Q: Is there anything I can do to prevent my Italian prune plums from falling off the tree in June?

A: There is nothing you can do to stop it and really you don't want to. Apples do the same thing; it is the tree's way of thinning its fruit to the crop it can handle with the number of leaves it has. Too many of your plums got pollinated and if they all stayed on the tree, they would be little tiny things.

With prune plums, you don't need to do any further thinning. With apples, the tree may still have too many fruits in some years and you might want to hand-thin further, remembering that an apple tree can handle one apple every four to six inches. Commercial orchards thin with a chemical spray because they have too many trees to thin by hand.

Q: I'm worried about thrips – how can I tell if I have them?

A: Go out to the garden with a piece of white paper in hand, hold the paper under the plant you think might have thrips and tap on the plant. Then check the paper and see if there are any thrips on it. They look like wee little black threads about as long as a poppy seed. That's awfully small, but they do show up on the paper.

If you have them in flowers, dust with diatomaceous earth. It has very sharp edges which stab the little critters and their vital juices leak out. Diatomaceous earth is ground up diatoms – fossilized marine animals. It is as fine as flour and feels smooth to your fingers, but has many fine sharp edges that puncture insect bodies.

This fall, be sure you thoroughly clean up all debris around all the plants that had thrips so they can't overwinter in the duff and infect next year's flowers. In the spring, drench the soil under those plants with a solution of insecticidal soap.

Glads are one flower often afflicted with thrips. To prevent an infestation, soak the corms in a solution of one T. of Lysol to a half-gallon of water before planting them.

Q: I read in a book about verticillium wilt, but how do I know if that's what is turning my plant leaves yellow?

A: Without a second thought you know that is not your problem.

Verticillium wilt does not turn leaves yellow – the plant just dies – almost instantly. When you have a plant that looked healthy one afternoon and the next morning is a wilted heap on the ground, you suspect verticillium wilt.

If half the plant suddenly collapses and half looks healthy, you can be quite sure it is verticillium wilt. For reasons unknown, it sometimes attacks only part of a plant.

It is a very common fungus in the western United States. It lives in the soil and, basically, there is no treatment for it.

All plants are not attacked by verticillium. If you look at a tomato seed packet, there will usually be some initials after the variety name, one of which may be V, indicating that the plant is verticillium-resistant. (You may also see F, N or C, indicating resistance to fusarium wilt, nematodes and cold. Although fusarium wilt is common in the east, it is almost unknown here, and nematodes are not one of our problems, either.)

If you have a plant die of verticillium wilt, you know that for several years you should plant in that place only the kind of plants that don't get wilt at all or the varieties that you know are verticillium resistant.

Verticillium kills the way most fungal diseases do, by plugging up the internal plumbing system of the plant. That's why it dies so quickly. It is as if it had suddenly experienced a deadly drought.

Verticillium wilt is probably the most common fungus infection in the western United States and a lot of scientists are looking for solutions to the problem. Recent studies at the University of California at Davis used ground up cabbage, broccoli and cauliflower, which seem to resist the wilt, to spread on the soil before planting eggplant seedlings. They tested the slop both fresh and after it was dried. All three vegetables worked to some extent, but broccoli showed the best results – 80 percent less verticillium wilt than the control plot.

Q: We live near a river bottom and the bagworms seem to come out of that area. What can I use to control them? A neighbor said Safer is a joke – it doesn't get anything.

A: Bt will kill bagworms. We have done it and know it works. It stands for Bacillus thuringiensis and it kills only caterpillars. If you hit the caterpillar, Bt will kill the caterpillar. If it is eating the plants (for instance, a cabbage worm caterpillar) and you don't hit the caterpillar, Bt will kill the caterpillar when it eats the leaves. Bt will not kill honeybees, lady bugs, spiders, cats, dogs or other desirable things.

When you ask for Bt, a lot of clerks will tell you they have never heard of it, but it is sold under several brand names, including Dipel, Thuricide and Caterpillar Killer. The last trade name is Bt manufactured by Safer.

You said your neighbor thinks Safer is a joke and doesn't kill anything. However, Safer is a manufacturer's name and not a product. That's like saying Ortho is a joke.

Safer does make some of the less toxic products, for the control of both insects and weeds. We don't know which one your neighbor didn't like, but it wouldn't have been Bt, which is very effective.

You have to know first of all that Bt kills only caterpillars, so it is of no help with aphids. The other thing you need to know is that the caterpillars don't die instantly. They die just as dead, but it takes them between one and three days to get there. This time lapse is not a problem. Bt kills by paralyzing the caterpillar's gut and although the caterpillar does not die immediately, it does stop eating immediately.

We have been told you can kill bagworms with diazinon, by spreading a band of it where they will walk across it. We have not personally tried it. We don't know what happens with diazinon but we have testimonials from gardeners who have used Bt and not had to spray again for several years.

Diazinon has the disadvantage of killing the good guys as well as the bad guys, and there are more guys with white hats out there in the garden than the ones with black hats.

That's why wide-spectrum insecticides fix your immediate problem, but create a worse one in the long run by killing the good bugs you didn't even know were there eating the bad bugs.

Remember, you can kill bagworms only when they are on the move. Nothing will reach them when they are sealed in their mud huts. Those which are not moving are often dead – just empty cases. When they are in a place like on your house, if you can stand to leave them for a year or two, when you remove them they are less likely to take the paint with them. You have to wait for the glue to break down, and a lot of people can't bear to wait that long.

Q: I keep trying to grow clematis on the south side of my house and they do fine, but always die in the winter. Should I give up?

A: No, just plant on a different side of the house. Even though the clematis seems to do fine for one summer on the south, if you don't have a lot of shade there, it probably isn't flourishing as it would on the east or west side. Clematis here does better with half-day than full-day sun. Like lilies, it likes its face in the sun and its feet in the shade, but if you can furnish a bit of shade in the summer and mulch heavily in winter to keep it frozen, it might still survive on the south.

Recipes for what to do with a plant don't work as well as understanding what a plant's needs are and trying to provide for them in your particular situation.

An east wall is ideal for clematis because it will get the same number of hours of sun as it would on the west but the sun comes in the cooler morning hours and the clematis won't have a hot building bouncing the heat back onto it. But whatever its exposure, it is important to keep its roots cool. This can be done by mulching heavily or by planting annuals around it. The bottom of the vine is not particularly lovely and the annuals will be big enough to be shading the ground by the time things really heat up in the summer.

We have good luck with a clematis planted on a west wall with foxglove around it. Be sure when you choose a plant to put by your clematis you don't pick something too vigorous and that it's not planted too close.

Currently we are trying a trick used in England where they let vines scramble up or through a tree or shrub. We don't know if it is going to work in this climate, but last year we planted a clematis on the north side of a caragana. It's too early for long-term prognostication, but the clematis has looked very healthy for three years. The idea is to give the clematis something to climb on and to pair it with a supporting tree or shrub that blooms at a different time of the year.

Q: I have grown sweet peas in the same place for years. This year, because of some renovation on the house, I planted them in the same place but in a wooden trough planter. I thought they would be happy, but they look terrible. How can I grow sweet peas again?

Q: What's wrong with my white rose? It's in a container and the plant looks OK, but it doesn't bloom. It has had eight buds, but only one opened. The others just dried up and fell off.

A: The basic problem in both cases is that the plants are in containers. When you have a lot of hot days, the soil in the containers has gotten too hot. Most plants can stand a lot of heat as long as their roots are cool.

The less insulation the container provides, the hotter the soil will get. When you container-garden, you want to use an insulated container, a double container or a shaded container. There are some very nice looking, decorative containers on the market now made of a very dense Styrofoam, and they work. They are treated to remain stable in ultraviolet rays of sunlight so they don't disintegrate the first year.

Wood offers some insulation value but it takes a pretty good-sized wood planter to keep a soil mass cool – a half-barrel will do pretty well, but a trough won't because the amount of soil in it is so small. In addition, the soil in a trough is not really deep enough to satisfy the requirements of sweet peas – you want at least five inches of soil. The bigger the container, the bigger the soil mass and the easier it is to keep the soil cool. It is much easier to grow in a 16-inch pot than in a six-inch pot.

With these containers, you can get through the rest of the season by using something for shade. Just leaning a board up against the side of the pot helps, although you may not want just any old board decorating your patio or front yard. With the rose container you can create a double pot just by setting one pot inside a larger one. The empty space between the pot walls provides shade, or you can fill the space with something like Styrofoam peanuts. With both the rose and the sweet peas, remember to shade the top of the soil with an inch or two of any kind of organic mulch.

Q: I got a miniature rose bush for Mother's Day. It has already stopped blooming and the leaves are falling off. Is there any hope?

A: It is possible you have a rose for which nothing can be done. Some nurseries are potting three or four cuttings to a pot and forcing them into bloom for specific occasions like Mother's Day or Valentine's Day. These are programmed to die.

To see if this is your situation, tip the plant out of the pot and see if it has a normal-looking root system or if there are just three or four cubes in there.

Most miniature roses are not happy in the house. One of the quality miniature rose growers will guarantee their plants 100 percent, If you do not try to keep them in the house.

If you find that your plant has a good root system, try putting it outdoors, but make the transition gradual. Set it in the shade for a few days.

Don't leave it out at night for the first three nights. At the end of a week, plant it in the ground in full sun or as nearly full sun as you can manage.

Miniature roses usually have a flush of bloom about every six weeks.

Roses, even the little ones, are heavy feeders. Assuming it survives, fertilize it once a month. (If it doesn't survive, it doesn't need to be fed.)

It takes a week or two for things like these symptoms to show up, so the rose might just be telling you that two weeks ago you let it get too wet or too dry. You could have done everything right since then. You may not be able to save it, but there is a chance; since it was a gift, you probably want to make the effort.

If it lives, prune your little rose the same way you would a hybrid tea or it will get straggly. You can cut it back any time to just above any leaf stem with five leaflets on it. It won't mind at all and will keep a nicer shape.

This winter, mulch it thoroughly. It may or may not survive. Some minis are hardier than others, and their survival depends more on the rose than it does on its winter treatment.

Q: Why do the garden books say not to hoe or cultivate around corn?

A: Corn plants have shallow root systems, but they also have "prop" roots. These are roots made to hold up something tall and heavy. You can see them around the bottom of the stalk, growing down into the soil. So hoeing or tilling around the plants threatens the plant's physical stability, as well as its feeding system.

A national vegetable? Corn is probably Americans' favorite vegetable, but in Europe, it is still looked upon with considerable suspicion. Europeans have been growing field corn for a very long time. They call it "cow corn." During World War II, when there were severe food shortages in Europe, cow corn became a staple and they got thoroughly sick of it. If you have never tasted field corn, we can assure you that you would be sick of it shortly, too. It is starchy, tough and not at all sweet. However, if it is picked green, it is edible. You just have to know exactly when to pick it – the palatability window is a mere peephole.

Q: I have a slug problem. I have spread bait, but it hasn't done any good. Is there a better way?

A: Better, yes. More fun, no.

We still favor hand-picking in flower and vegetable beds and greenhouses. Slugs are particularly fond of baby lettuce and will devour the tiny plants in their entirety. Before setting lettuce out, it must be big enough to grow faster than a slug can eat.

You can trap slugs under boards, asphalt shingles or grapefruit rinds. Of course, you still have to pick them up and dispatch them by your choice of methods.

Diatomaceous earth sprinkled around the plants you want to protect can be effective – we have used it around strawberries. (The only thing worse than picking a strawberry a slug has eaten a hole in is picking one in which he's still in the hole eating.) However, diatomaceous earth is only effective when dry and must be reapplied after rain.

You can set out beer in traps that your slugs might prefer to your flowers and vegetables. Some people say slugs like the more expensive beers best, but others say sugar water works just as well as beer. A new slug bait, which uses iron phosphate, has been put out because the slime balls are becoming resistant to metaldehyde, the common active ingredient in the old ones.

In Britain, they don't think the problem is slugs becoming resistant. They did experiments with different dosages of metaldehyde. At less than six percent in the bait, very few died, especially in cool, damp weather. At eight percent, 70 percent survived. So the Brits concluded that the metaldehyde was making the slugs just sick enough to ruin their appetites; they stopped eating before ingesting a fatal dose.

Q: I seem to remember your saying one should stop fertilizing at some point in the summer. Are we there yet?

A: The first of August is the time to stop feeding all your perennials. You don't want them to make tender new growth when it wouldn't have time to toughen up before frost. The annuals, however, are a different matter. They will appreciate a little snack about once a month until they quit.

Q: The instructions I have for drying oregano say to pick it just before the flowers open. Do you dry the flowers with the rest of it?

A: No. The flowers won't add anything to the taste of your spaghetti sauce. Quite the contrary.

However, it's a good idea to pick off the blossoms whether you are planning to dry the leaves or not. This is true of any herb. As soon as a plant blooms, it's pretty much finished for culinary purposes. As soon as buds appear, take them off. That way, you will get at least some more new leaves, which is the part of the plant you want.

Q: I told my neighbor the June drop was over and it was time to thin her apples. She said I was crazy. Am I?

A: Neither of you needs to call in a psychiatrist just yet.

It is not absolutely necessary to thin apples and if you have very many trees, you obviously won't. But if you have only a few, you would be wise to do it.

There are two main reasons. First, you will get fewer, bigger apples. There is no particular advantage to having a huge crop of golf-ball-size apples.

Second, thinning will keep your tree from entering an alternate-bearing cycle. If it produces too many apples one year, it exhausts its head of steam, and next year it will still be recovering. We have enough difficulty getting a crop because of the weather around here without contributing more problems ourselves.

If you are going to thin, plan to leave four to six inches between apples. This should leave your tree with enough leaves to properly nourish each apple.

Q: What does "pinching out" mean?

A: This is the pruning you do with your thumb and index finger. It is the best kind of pruning because you are taking off the tender, small pieces without the use of tools. You are not cutting off big chunks that the plant has just spent a lot of energy growing.

You do it to fast-growing plants to maintain a nice shape. When you pinch out a plant, it branches where it was pinched.

Q: I read that wood ashes were good for your garden, and since I had an area of mine that had not been doing well, I put wood ashes on it. This year, nothing at all will grow there. What did I do wrong? Is it fixable?

A: The article you read was written for a different part of the country. Wood ashes are an excellent source of potassium, but our soils don't need additional potassium as those of the Northeast do. You can have too much of any nutrient. Too much potassium keeps the plants from using available nitrogen and magnesium. The ashes also may have made your soil too alkaline.

Do three things: 1. Stop putting wood ashes on your garden. 2. Spread around the ashy soil that's there already. 3. Add compost and ash-free soil to the area.

We don't know why your plants weren't doing well there in the first place, but it wasn't a lack of potassium.

Q: I have a lovely rose I'd like to have more of, but I can't seem to find one. Is it possible to propagate a new bush from this old favorite?

A: It probably is, but there are a couple of caveats. First, if it's a patented rose, you can't do that. That's not fair. Somebody has spent a lot of money and a whole lot of time developing it; they are entitled to recoup by charging a fee to others who propagate their rose.

You can't just say, "That's a great, huge, rich company and they'll never miss it." It's not and they would. The work is mostly done by individuals or very small companies.

If a rose is patented, it will say so on its little metal tag. Or the tag could say, "P.P. R." which means, "patent privilege reserved."

If it's a very old rose, you need not worry. Rose patents last only 17 years.

A second consideration is whether your rose is grafted. If you're dealing with tender roses like hybrid teas, they are grafted on a hardy rootstock, although others may be grown on their own roots.

If your bush does not fit either of these categories, you can propagate it by rooting a cutting. Clip off a shoot that has recently bloomed. Cut off the blossom and the first leaf, leaving a cutting four to six inches long. Clip leaves from the bottom half.

You can't root the top end of the cutting, and sometimes it is very difficult to tell which end is which, once the flower is gone. Propagators – especially those doing a lot of cuttings – cut them straight across on top and at an angle at the bottom.

Dip the stem in a rooting compound. These products are hormones that encourage root growth and also have some antifungal properties.

If the stem is dry, dip it in water first so the powder will stick. You need to have some rooting compound a bit above the soil level.

Place the treated cutting in a pot deep enough to allow roots to grow down. Use individual four-inch pots if rooting only a few cuttings. For a lot, use a flat at least three inches deep.

Fill the container with sterile starting mix. Make a hole with a pencil so you can insert the stem without wiping off the powder. Firm the soil around it and water. Cover with plastic to ensure high humidity. This plant has no roots and will die on you if it gets dry.

Place the container in good light, but not in the sun. If you've got a place outdoors, bury the bottom of the pot a half-inch or so in the ground to keep it from drying.

The cutting should have roots in a month or two. If the leaves die, it's not going to do anything. If it's going to grow, it will have made new growth. To check, either tug gently on the stem or turn the pot over, tip the dirt ball out and look for roots. Rooting takes a while.

For its first winter, put your plant into another pot filled with potting soil or a mixture of potting and garden soils. Keep it in a sheltered place, below freezing but not where it will get to 20 below zero. If you have a garage or unheated crawl space, put it to sleep there. Light doesn't matter, since the rose is dormant. If you have treated it well and it likes you, it might even bloom next year.

Q: When I am digging in the garden and find grubs, do I kill them or leave them?

A: When in doubt, opt for mercy. If you don't know that it is bad, let it live. The number and kind of insects that are beneficial are greater than those that aren't. Only about a half a dozen in any garden are harmful. By far the most numerous are those that are neutral, and even those may do good things, like pollinate for you. They may not eat up bad bugs and may have a very small effect, but anything they do will be positive.

When you squash something you don't know, you are much more likely to be killing something with friendly fire than shooting down an enemy.

Q: My husband just brought home some asparagus roots and we don't know where to plant them. We have a very limited garden space. He is leaning toward planting them next to the raspberries. Would this be all right?

A: Choose another spot. The raspberries will send up suckers among the asparagus roots and you'll never get them separated. Plant the asparagus next to an annual crop so that at least once a year you will be able to dig up the weeds and grass near it. Once you have a grass problem, all you can do is dig up the asparagus.

Don't worry about how many years to wait before cutting your first spears. Just don't harvest anything smaller than a lead pencil and quit cutting on the Fourth of July. Period. How many spears you get next year is a factor of how many ferns grow on your plants this year.

Q: I got a few red geraniums a month ago. They are blooming fine, but the bottom leaves are turning yellow. Am I keeping them too wet? They are in pots in full sun.

A: Maybe. They could also be too dry. The trouble is that too wet and too dry produce the same symptoms. Dry is more likely for potted plants on a south side on sunny days.

Although they do love sunny weather, geraniums don't want their roots to boil, so shade the south side of the pots.

A plant blooming in a pot is probably rootbound and needs to drink fairly often, but geraniums like to dry out between waterings. Pick up the pot once a day and wait to water it until it feels lighter than the last time.

Or you can poke a finger into the soil and if the top inch is dry, water it.

If you can't bear to poke your fingers into dirt, plant plastic geraniums.

Q: What can I put in the pots against a red brick wall on my deck where it gets extremely hot?

A: Basically, annuals are going to be easier than perennials because perennials don't winter over well in pots. They freeze too solidly and dry out. It takes a very large container for them to survive.

Among the annuals, plants that originated in hot areas of the world will be happiest, including the composites from South Africa like gazania. Be sure you plant sun-worshipers, as opposed to shade lovers. A great many annuals will do very well, but stay away from ones with large, thin leaves, like petunias, which lose a lot of water through their expanse of leaf surface. Those with smaller and/or thicker leaves don't breathe quite so fast, and it's easier for the roots to keep up with them.

Taking care of the roots is the vital thing. Most flowers will stand an awful lot of heat as long as their roots stay cool and damp. This is easiest to do if you use big containers because the dirt in small pots will heat up much faster than that in a large tub.

There are several ways to insulate your plants' roots. You can use a container with intrinsic insulating value, like wood or molded Styrofoam. If the container itself is not insulated, line it with an inch or so of scrap Styrofoam before adding the potting soil. Put a mulch on top of the dirt so the sun doesn't bake the roots. You can mulch with organic material like grass clippings or wood chips, or use a two-inch layer of pebbles or rocks.

Even well insulated container plants in the conditions you describe will have to be watered every single day – some days perhaps twice.

Your containers probably will look prettiest with a mixture of plants in them, rather than one type per pot. Try to include a spike, a ball and a creeper. You might use one foliage plant, like an ornamental grass or one of several kinds of herbs, with a couple of flowering plants.

There are so many good choices of plants that we prefer to give basic principles instead of a list of varieties to plant. Just keep these suggestions in mind when you go to the nursery to buy your plants, then see what's available and which you like best. Then insulate, mulch and water, water, water.

Q: How can you tell a flower seedling from a weed?

A: The first ones up are likely to be weeds. When the flowers do come up, a lot will poke through at the same time and the location will tell you something. You can't identify many weeds from their seed leaves and must wait until they have four or five true leaves to see what it is going to be when it grows up.

If you are in doubt, leave it. Unless you let it flower and set seeds, it won't hurt to let a weed grow until you can be sure you're not pulling up one of your fledgling flowers.

Once you know you have flower seedlings, you must thin mercilessly. Leave one plant, not a group of seedlings, and leave eight inches between plants. Otherwise, you end up with a forest of skinny, tall plants with small flowers because the plants can't bush out.

Eight inches looks like a whole lot of empty space when you first do your thinning. If you cannot bear this, thin once to four inches apart, then when they get too big, take out half.

Q: Something is eating holes along the edges of the leaves of my roses. I tried diazinon, but it didn't help. What is it and what can I do?

A: Leaf-cutter bees are causing the damage. No spray controls them. The bees are not eating the leaf. They just cut out pieces and use them to make their nests. This only goes on for a couple of weeks. If it really bugs you, cover the roses for a week or two with floating row cover or fine netting or any physical barrier.

All insects behave in extremely habitual ways. If they come around for a few days and can't get to your roses, they will go to another plant. It may not be one of yours. We don't know what the arrangement is between the insects and the plants, but the bees never take enough to harm the plant.

Q: My lawn looks terrible! I can't get the water around fast enough to avoid brown spots. Isn't there something I can do?

A: There are two things. First, if you don't already have your mower blades on their highest setting, get 'em there. This is especially important when the weather is hot and dry. The longer grass can act as a living mulch, shading the soil and conserving water.

Second, stop moving the water around as fast as you can. You want to water slowly and deeply. There's no way to keep the top inch of soil damp anyway. What you need is grass with nice, long roots. To achieve that, you need to let the grass work a little bit for water all season long. Give it a big drink and then let it dry out. With this regimen in place, you shouldn't have to water more than once a week.

How much water do you give it? It needs an inch a week in not more than two batches. To measure, put a coffee can on the lawn halfway out the distance the sprinkler is going to go. Note the time and turn on the sprinkler. When you get to the desired amount, check the clock to see how long it took you to deliver enough water. In hot weather, it is more likely to be eight hours than two. This amount will vary from one sprinkler to another, so measure each type. Don't forget any automatic sprinklers you have operating.

If you don't have a sprinkler system, buy a timer. Get a good one. With a reliable timer, you can set it for the desired length of watering and go off to work without worry.

Q: I get conflicting advice about my lawn care and I'm not sure my lawn service is doing the right things. At what height should it be cut? Should they be using a mulching blade?

A: For quite a few years, experts have recommended a mowing height of two and one-half inches. Recently, they have revised the figure to three inches in hot weather.

When grass is left a bit longer, it shades the ground better, conserving moisture. Grass is healthier when it doesn't have to contend with drought stress. The shading effect probably also prevents the germination or survival of at least some weeds and quackgrass.

In any event, healthy grass is wonderful at choking out weeds. Mow often enough that you don't have to take off more than a third of the length at once. In spring and fall, this usually works out to be once a week. In mid-summer when it's hot and the grass is not growing as fast, it will probably be every other week.

Experts now agree on the value of mulching mowers. They consider the mulchers a great improvement over the older types.

The purpose of a mulching blade is to chop up the clippings and distribute them evenly over the lawn, thus returning nitrogen directly to the soil. But you can't let the grass get six inches high before mowing. The blade can't handle that much volume and it spits out globs of clippings, which have to be raked up.

The advice on fertilizing is to do it very little or not at all. Without fertilizing, you won't have to mow as often and you won't be contributing to the buildup of undesirable thatch.

Q: If I keep the weeds cut so they don't go to seed, do I have to burn the cuttings?

A: No. If they haven't gone to seed, just compost them. The exception to this is purslane. You don't have to burn it, but it must be dried out – on top of black plastic or on the driveway, or any place the sun will get it.

Purslane plants have enough moisture stored to enable them to produce viable seeds even after being cut or pulled. Also, if the plants are placed on soil, they will root down again.

Some perennial weeds – like thistles – have underground stolons that allow them to spread even if the tops are cut off, but at least you will prevent them from spreading by seed.

Q: I started perennial sweet peas last year and they are blooming beautifully. I have been cutting the spent flowers. When should I stop cutting them off and allow them to go to seed?

A: It doesn't matter, unless you want to start a lot more. Some perennials bloom longer if the faded blossoms are removed, but not sweet peas. Some perennials will make a second bloom if you cut the seed pods off and some won't. Sweet peas won't.

There are some perennials you don't want to go to seed. Veronica and achillea, for instance, reseed freely and spread all over the place.

Annuals are different. The purpose of annuals is to make seeds. So if you cut off the old blooms, they keep on trying. If you don't, they think they have succeeded and quit blooming. With annual sweet peas it is very important to cut off the pods to keep them flowering. With your perennials, you just have to decide how many you want and how you want your plants to look.

Q: Why aren't my nasturtiums blooming? The foliage is healthy and profuse. I see them in window boxes all over town with scant foliage and many blossoms. Why?

A: You are probably just too nice to them. With nitrogen-rich soil, they grow great leaves.

You might try putting them in containers – not too large – and not fertilizing them. Eventually, the soil will run low on nitrogen and they will start blooming.

This peculiar behavior probably has to do with heritage.

Nasturtiums are one of only a handful of flowers that bloom well in poor soil.

If you don't have access to any poor soil, you could plant a variety called Alaska. They have variegated foliage so nice that you might not even care if they bloom.

Q: Why did the buds fall off my pepper plants?

A: Pepper plants won't set any more fruits than they can support. Their solution is just to let the buds fall.

However, blossom drop also would happen if the plants got too dry, too hot or too cold. Peppers are notorious for dropping blossoms if it gets over 90 degrees or under 50.

One thing you can do is to buy only the varieties of peppers bred for this area. Look for wording like "for cooler climates," or "less cold-sensitive."

Q: What is eating my currants? It skeletonizes the leaves and then starts eating the fruit. I don't want to use anything poisonous because there are small children in the neighborhood.

A: Imported currant worms are eating your currants. That's their official name. Of course it was the worms, not the currants, which were imported, and we assume it was accidental.

If you haven't seen them and want to, look for a green or greenish-blue caterpillar that may have black spots or a black head. Imported currant worms really can defoliate the bushes, but there is comforting news. The good old Bt *(Bacillus thuringiensis)* we keep recommending takes care of them. By three days after treatment, the worms will be dry and hard.

Bt is a natural bacterium which won't hurt the kids or their parents or their pets or the ladybugs or the birds. It attacks only caterpillars and works by paralyzing the gut. To get to the gut, it has to be ingested, so it won't even kill a caterpillar unless it's eating a leaf – or currant – to which it has been applied.

It is widely available from local nurseries and garden supply departments under several brand names. If you ask for it and the clerk gives you a blank look, just try another store.

Bt is good for stopping the little green worms on your cabbages, broccoli, cauliflower and Brussels sprouts. There are even special types for special creatures, like Bt san diego for potato beetle larvae.

The current recommendation for currant worms is to apply it, whether in a spray or as dust, just before sundown or on a cloudy day because it breaks down fairly fast in bright sunlight. Also, it seems to be less effective when mixed in alkaline water, so if you have that kind, add a dash of vinegar to the water before putting in the Bt.

Q: Do you buy ladybugs?

A: No. We just invite them in.

The kind you would buy would probably be *Hippodamia convergens*. This is a western species that winters in huge groups, usually high on mountains (like St. Mary's Peak in the Bitterroots), making them easy to collect for people selling ladybugs.

However, they are more likely to help someone else than you. They wake up thinking they are still in the mountains and fly straight up, waiting for the wind to carry them off.

One man who does buy ladybugs told us he stores them in the refrigerator, where they will keep about a month. He releases a few at a time every other day just before dark. That way they have the dusk and the dark to eat before they start home – wherever that is – the next morning.

In the United States there are 475 species of ladybugs. The red ones eat aphids and the dark ones like whiteflies, mealybugs and scale. They are not native, but a wonderful example of an imported insect that was a success, rather than a disaster.

You may have read about invasions of ladybugs in the east and southeast. This is *Harmonia axyridis*. They were imported from Asia about 20 years ago to eat pecan aphids. They disappeared for about 10 years and then began to reappear. They clump like ours do, but instead of doing so in the mountains, they use houses. Nobody really minds much because they were a big success with the pecan aphids.

Not only do ladybugs eat bad insects, but their larvae – which are larger than the adults – do too. The larvae are orange and black or orange and blue, about half an inch long, and have bumps. They remind us of dragons.

Q: My neighbor says not to pull lettuce plants, but to cut them and they will grow back. Is that true?

A: Yes, it's true, but at the stage in its life cycle when lettuce wants to make seed, the leaves will become bitter.

The method is called "cut and come again." The chief advantage is that you don't thin your crop. Just plant it and let it come up as it will, beginning harvest in two to three weeks. The disadvantage is that the leaves are small. Sprinklers or a lot of rain will produce many small, dirty leaves, which translates into a lot of washing between garden and salad bowl.

Another way is to thin the plants when they are about two inches tall to one plant at least nine inches from its nearest neighbor. That way you get big heads with big, clean leaves. The disadvantage is having to thin and do it early. You have to thin to only ONE plant, not a group.

This is a good area for a great many kinds of lettuce. Even in midsummer you can plant lettuce as long as plants are in the shade. If you plant pinches of seed every nine inches, it simplifies thinning.

IN PRAISE OF EARTHWORMS – You probably know that earthworms are a primary aerator of garden soil and make it possible for your plant roots to grow deeper, but do you realize how much fertilizer they can provide?

They first help out your lawn by eating up thatch, but then bacteria in their guts turn this stuff into worm castings, which contain most of the essential plant nutrients, plus enormous quantities of beneficial micro organisms. Worm castings are terrific fertilizer.

If you have a healthy worm population, your soil is going to get up to a pound of worm castings per square foot, which amounts to about $25 worth on today's market.

If worms are making your lawn bumpy and you can't stand it, roll the area a couple – or three – times a season. Also, irrigating deeply and infrequently makes the lawn smoother because the worms stay down deeper. Worms can go as deep as nine feet.

Q: My juniper is about to take over the yard. It looks like the woods out of Hansel and Gretel. How do I contain it?

A: There are a couple of ways to deal with overgrown conifers and summer is the ideal time to tackle the task. One method is ruthless pruning and the other involves controlling new growth. Junipers are the conifers most likely to go for this harsh treatment and arbor vitae are next.

When you have a juniper that has been taken over by sparrows because even the cat can't get in to get at them, it's time to don a tough, long-sleeved shirt and leather gloves and cut your way into it with pruning shears. It is an extraordinarily prickly job.

Start at the bottom and get rid of the branches that are on the grass. Carve yourself an adit so you can get to the center. Your object will be to make a trunk for the shrub, and sooner or later you will come to that one big stem that goes all the way to the ground.

Cut the bottom branches off in the same way you would prune any tree, leaving the bark collar on the trunk. While you are in there, get rid of all the dead stuff, remove the mouse nests and retrieve the toy fire truck your son lost eight years ago.

This done, you will be able to look around and see which remaining branches are mostly dead and be able to clip them off. Take off any with only a little green. Eventually, you can crawl out again, stand up and see what things look like. You may be pleasantly surprised.

If you see things that still need removing, do it. Look for any branch sticking out, ruining the shape. You are more likely to cut off too little than too much, but remember that what you cut off this year will grow out again next. You aren't going to do any permanent damage. Stop when it looks good.

To create an oriental-looking shrub, you can take off everything except the green out at the branch tips.

For additional help in pruning, we recommend a video, "Pruning Your Own Shrubs and Small Trees," produced by the Agricultural Communications Center at the University of Idaho in 1987. It is still on the market, or you might be able to find a source from which to borrow it. It can be very helpful to see an expert demonstrating the techniques.

If your aim is to slow down the growth of a conifer and control its shape, you can do so by removing part of its candles, the light-green new growth at the tips of all the branches. The Japanese method is to put on a pair of gloves and break off part of each candle. They do this even with enormous trees, using a long ladder. The Japanese are very patient with their gardens.

If you want to slow down the growth a lot, break off three quarters of the candles. When there is a cluster of candles, break off all but one and break off part of that one.

What you are doing is slowing the tree down by removing part of the new year's growth, but it is important not to take it all off. You can always take off more next year. You are dealing with a long-term project – a tree.

If you are feeling more American than Japanese, you can use a hedge trimmer or pruning shears. Remember that the best job does not make you think about the pruning that must have been done – only what a lovely shape the tree or shrub is.

Q: What's making my tomato leaves curl under? I can't see any insects, but someone told me it could be mites.

A: This is called leaf roll and is purely physiological. There is no fungus and no insect involved and it is not harmful. It seems to be the tomato's reaction to environmental stress – cold wind, hot sun, drought, wet soil. The plant is probably trying to reduce stress by reducing the leaf surface exposed to it. When the weather changes and the stress lessens, the leaf curl will go away.

Q: I have heard the term "IPM" bandied about among gardening acquaintances, but I'm not sure just what it means. What do the letters stand for?

A: IPM stands for integrated pest management. That is a fancy name for "use common sense and think for yourself and you'll get along better."

Almost all the insects anywhere in your landscape are doing no damage to your plants. Of those that might be casting a gustatory glance at your gaillardia, most will be eaten up by predators that feed on them before they have a chance to hurt anything.

Insects are a big food source for such creatures as birds, skunks, frogs and toads, spiders, daddy-longlegs, and dragonflies, which eat almost nothing but insects.

The smallest insect predators you probably don't even notice. Some physically eat insects smaller than themselves. Others parasitize other insects, laying eggs in them, and when they hatch, the larvae eat the host from the inside. There are still smaller life forms, like viruses, bacteria and fungi, which live on insects.

But things can get out of hand and out of balance.

The guiding principal of IPM is to think about what you are trying to do – what you need to get rid of and how you can best accomplish that without upsetting the balance any further. The last thing you want to do is kill off something that is trying to help you by eating up the insects doing the damage.

IPM is not an esoteric system designed by eco-freaks. It is just a method to get balance back, for the least amount of work, in order to keep your garden healthy.

Sometimes this requires more time in pre-planning, but it will probably save a lot of time in the long run. You will spend more time planning than you would reaching for a spray can, but you won't have to keep reaching for the can.

The longer you practice IPM the less time you need to spend on pest control. The middle initial could well stand for patience. IPM doesn't mean you'll ever get to the point where you never have a problem, it just means that your problems will keep getting smaller.

The first step in IPM is to prevent damage by planting a variety of flowers and vegetables, which always gives you a healthier landscape than a monoculture. You may also switch variety, say from a monarda devoured by grasshoppers to a strain 'hoppers don't like. Plant the varieties that are least damaged in your garden.

Next, employ physical control – squash slugs, put in a barrier, cover plants with floating row cover. The point is to think about the problem and do something before it happens, if possible.

Sometimes, no matter what, you get damage and want to spray something. Start with something that will kill the fewest things possible. Bt (Bacillus thuringiensis) in various forms is very specific. Horticultural oils and insecticidal soaps get most soft-bodied insects. Among botanical insecticides are neem and pyrethrum. Diatomaceous earth is a natural deterrent.

There are cases when we feel you are justified in dragging out the big guns. We know of nothing but diazanon that will get raspberry cane borers. However, at the first sign of holes in your rose leaves, don't go out and squirt everything with diazanon. You will not kill one leaf-cutter bee but you will destroy a great many beneficial insects.

Instead of spraying first and asking questions later, begin by assessing the situation – who's doing the damage and how much of it can you put up with? Then start figuring out your best line of defense.

If your baby broccoli seedlings are getting lopped off at the ground, you must know a cutworm is at work. Since he kills the young plants so efficiently, you need to get rid of him. To prevent further damage, you would try a physical barrier first – like wrapping the stems in something the cutworm couldn't eat through. Unless you had acres of broccoli, you'd get out there, dig around the recently ruined plants, find the culprit and kill it.

It would take longer to figure out it was a cutworm, take steps to keep it off your plants, find its ugly body and smash it than it would to squirt the broccoli patch with diazinon, but wide spectrum insecticides are expensive, indiscriminate and many times ineffective. You would probably have killed some helpful beetles but not the cutworm.

In another scenario, if a few slugs are lunching on your lettuce and you are willing to discard outer leaves because of the slug holes, that you can live with. Perfect control is extremely expensive.

Another facet of your IPM plan could be planting as ornamentals things that are least susceptible to pests. An all-around healthy garden is best able to resist pest attacks. If you are a vegetable gardener, plant some flowers out there to encourage the beneficial insects you want to attract.

When you do get some bug eating up something, unless it's an emergency, wait a few days and see what happens. Aphids can wait, but if army worms are eating up your apple leaves, something has to be done immediately. Bt is not instant death, but usually the pest stops eating. So if you see caterpillars after you spray Bt, don't say, "Why isn't he dead?" Ask yourself, "Is he eating?"

IPM is a long-term project. After doing it for a year or two you will see you have been helping yourself because the population of beneficials will have built up. The only prerequisite of an IPM program is that you have to be smarter than the bug.

Fall

FALL

Q: We have pears on our tree this year for the first time, but I'm not sure how to tell when they are ripe enough to pick. Is there something to look for?

A: What is important is not to wait for them to get ripe on the tree. If you do, they will be rotting at the core. You must pick them green.

You tell when it's time to pick them by putting together a few things. Have they got full size? (Have they stopped getting bigger?) The color will have started to change. They will still be green, but the green will be getting lighter colored. It will not be too hard to pull them off the tree – they won't fall off in your hand, but you needn't give a mighty jerk.

Ripen them in the dark. Nobody's house has the kind of place that provides ideal ripening temperature for pears, so keep them at room temperature and check them every few days. Depending on how ripe they were when picked, it will be anywhere from a few days to a couple of weeks until they are ready to eat.

Q: I bought a tarragon plant but it turns out it wasn't really tarragon. This one didn't have any particular flavor at all. How can I tell when I buy it as a plant?

A: The plant probably is what's called Russian tarragon. French tarragon is *Artemisia dracunculus* var. *sativa*. Russian tarragon is var. *dracunculoides*. It looks quite a lot like French tarragon, but has no taste, or sometimes a mild and unpleasant taste. It is a bigger, more vigorous plant. How you can find out when buying a plant is to ask whether it was grown from seed. If the answer is yes, it is Russian tarragon. French tarragon very seldom flowers and never sets seed. It must be propagated by divisions.

If you like to grow your herbs from seed and see tarragon in a catalog, don't order it.

Q: I know you aren't supposed to let basil flower, but every time I pinch off the flower buds, it just grows more. Is there some secret?

Q: I wish I knew how to keep a basil plant growing. I know it isn't supposed to flower, so each time it does, I take out that plant. I have to keep starting basil plants all summer so I can have a supply.

A: It is possible to keep your basil pruned to keep it from flowering for a LONG time. You just have to know its one little secret. It is genetically programmed to flower at the end of any stem once it gets six pairs leaves. So if you pinch off just the flower, it will re-flower. Instead, cut that stem all the way back, leaving only the first pair of leaves. Usually the plant will grow two new stems at that point. It will make usable leaves until it gets up to six. When those two stems start to make flower buds, cut them back to the first pair of leaves, and so on. This doesn't go on ad infinitum, but the Montana isn't infinite summer either.

Basil's botanical name is *Ocimum basilicum*, which means "princely." It is half Greek, half Latin, with *Ocimum* coming from the Greek and *basilicum* from the Latin.

Basil has a long, long history. Nobody knows just how far back it goes, but at the time of Christ, it was known to both Greeks and Romans. It was used in French cooking as far back as the Middle Ages and was grown as a medicinal plant at least as early as 1600. It went out of fashion as a culinary herb, and was not much used in cooking until the basil boom started in this country about 1980.

The cultivars are all mixed up now and there are many types you can grow. A couple of herbalists grew 100 different varieties last year – 4,000 different plants. They were trying to sort out the names of things. They decided that not more than two-thirds of those varieties were truly different, but were the same plant under different names.

Among the types, sweet basil is the stuff that goes into pesto and other Italian cooking. There are many varieties, ranging from tiny leaves on tiny plants like "Green Globe" and "Green Bouquet," all the way up to enormous leaves on the variety called "lettuce leaved." There is also purple basil like "Purple Ruffles" or "Red Rubin." By now even the purple strains are no longer pure. You may get seeds or a plant, supposed to be purple, that turns out to have a whole lot of green leaves. The flavor is the same as the green varieties.

There are basils with different flavors. Probably the best known is lemon basil, *Ocimum x citriodorum*, which comes from Indonesia and is most often used in salads.

There is a cinnamon basil from Mexico. An anise or licorice basil has a strong flavor and sometimes has purple stems and leaves. (If you have a purple basil that doesn't taste like basil, that may be it.)

Sacred or holy basil, *O. sanctum*, is from India and has a spicy flavor that reminds us of huckleberries. But beware. A spicy basil, *O. americanum*, is sometimes sold as sacred basil. We bought seeds of it once, thinking that we had Indian sacred basil. This plant has hairy leaves and little pink flowers. We think it has a nasty smell, nothing like huckleberries.

Q: How do I save seeds from my nasturtiums and sweet peas? Should I gather them when the petals have fallen or wait until they are dry?

A: The answer is the same for both flowers. You must allow them to dry on the plant. If picked green, they won't mature, so leave them on the plant until the seed pods turn brown.

On some plants, the pods open rather explosively and spray the seeds around. That's how nature helps them expand their territory. The solution to that is to bag the seed head in something porous – a piece of nylon stocking, paper bag or cheese cloth. Just don't use plastic. The object is to allow them to mature and dry and still keep them from getting away from you.

With any plant from which you intend to collect seed, check the original seed packet and make sure it doesn't say it is a hybrid. If it is, the plants you get will be very different from the parents and the change will almost surely not be for the better.

Q: I have a lovely rosemary plant in the garden and hate to lose it to the coming cold. Can I bring it inside in a pot for the winter?

A: You can certainly bring it in, but don't blame yourself if it curls up its toes and dies anyway. Many garden plants have trouble adjusting to incarceration in a warmer, darker space.

Its chances will be best if it has lived in a pot outdoors so you won't have to weaken its resolve still further by digging it up, breaking a bunch of roots and cramming what's left into a pot it has never known.

Acclimate your plant on its way indoors over a period of a couple of weeks, just the reverse of hardening off seedlings on their way out of the house in the spring. Bring it in at night for a few days and gradually increase its indoor time.

Rosemary is a perennial in more temperate areas where it takes the winters in stride, but those sissy seasons don't qualify for the term "winter" here in Montana.

Q: The geraniums in my flowerbeds are still lovely and I want to bring them in and save them over the winter. Are there special things to do?

A: Moving geraniums from the ground to indoor pots requires a little different treatment from bringing in already-potted ones.

Recipes you may have read say to shake off as much dirt from the roots as possible, which strikes us as a particularly dumb rule. We don't offer recipes, but suggestions based on personal experience and preference.

Dig up the plants, giving them a root ball slightly smaller than the pot you're going to put them in, leaving dirt around the roots. This is easiest to do if the soil is damp, but not muddy.

In a pot you need lighter soil than the plant had outside, so once it's in the container, fill around it with an airy potting soil. Prune off some of the leaves right away. Your plant will have lost some roots in the transfer process and will need to lose some foliage to maintain its balance. Other than that, proceed as for all outdoor-to-indoor plants.

Another option for keeping geraniums for next year is to let them go dormant, rather than maintaining them as houseplants through the winter. They need to be put in a place that is cold, but above freezing – about 40 degrees is ideal. People who have crawl spaces under their houses have good luck keeping dormant geraniums there.

If you're digging up a geranium to send into dormancy, it doesn't matter what sort of soil you put in the pot. Check it a few times during the winter to see that it doesn't get bone dry.

Q: I dug up my tarragon and rosemary and brought them in the house, but they both died. Why wouldn't they grow on my windowsill?

A: The two probably died for different reasons.

Tarragon doesn't do well indoors because it is a temperate climate plant that requires a dormant season. However, it is quite tough.

Molly always left hers outside and mulched it every year. She felt rewarded when it came back every spring. Then she had a call from a woman in South Dakota who never covered hers at all and it still prospered. Although Molly's tarragon never seemed to mind its warm blankets, since that telephone call it has done just as well without the mulch.

The rosemary is a Mediterranean plant. We suspect that the articles we read about bringing herbs inside for the winter are written by people who have never done that. It is possible to bring some of them in, but a lot of times they just won't live.

When you dig your herbs out of the garden, you can't help destroying a lot of their root systems because they haven't been kept nice and compact. The plants are going to have to grow a lot of new roots, plus a whole new set of indoor leaves.

In addition, the garden soil is not suitable for potting, so you either have an unsuitable core surrounded by suitable potting soil or you must knock off an awful lot of soil – and roots – while working potting soil in around them.

When you bring plants in, their light and soil levels change. Their 40-degree daily temperature variations are suddenly reduced to five or ten degrees. Chances are, you are keeping your houseplants wetter than you did your herb garden. The poor things are hit with everything at the same time. The amazing thing is that ALL of them don't die.

At this time of year plants know winter is coming and they get ready for sleep – or at least semi-dormancy. It is not a good time to ask them to grow new leaves and roots.

If you want indoor-outdoor herbs, plant them in pots and leave them there. Introduce them to the outdoors gradually in the spring and to the indoors gradually in the fall. When you take them outside, dig a hole and set the pot in, leaving the rim just above the soil surface. This makes it easy to water and the roots keep cooler. Just be sure to pull the pot up or twist it around about once a week, or when you dig it up in the fall you will find a split pot and a root system well on its way to China.

To ensure the survival of your herbs, keep cuttings or divisions. This needed to be done in early August, when the plants were still growing well and not just before the first killing frost. You can try the technique next summer.

Q: I have a geranium in a hanging pot with another plant, whose name I can't remember. I'd like to bring it inside. How should I treat it?

A: The future of the second plant is uncertain, since its identity is unknown. We can't promise it will still be alive and well next spring. But if they got along all right outside all summer, maybe what's good for one will be good for the other – like sauce for geese and ganders and all that.

If your pot was hanging on a south or west side, give it the same exposure inside. If it had partial shade, hang it in an east window. Try to give the plants the morning light or all-day exposure they have been happy with.

Just being inside means they will be getting a lot less light than they had outdoors. As a result, the internodes will lengthen and continue to do so as the days grow shorter.

(In case you have forgotten about internodes, that just means that the leaves will be farther apart on the stems – the plant gets leggy.)

A happy plant has a balance of light, water and nutrients. When you bring the pot inside, you can't do anything about the reduced light, but you can maintain the balance by reducing the water and nutrients. Keep the soil a little on the dry side but not drought-stricken. Fertilize it more lightly, but not less often.

There is no need to repot your plant, but prune off anything that looks ugly. Most blooming plants will continue for quite a while after moving indoors if they are reasonably happy. Don't worry if they drop quite a few leaves. They will be making new ones. The outdoor leaves are tough and thick-skinned to deal with Montana weather. The new ones will be more tender and thin-skinned to deal with living room weather.

If you have the option, try to move the plants indoors gradually, bringing them in at night for a few days, giving them less outside time over a week or so.

Q: What should I do to leave my lawn in the best shape for winter? Should I mow it short? Should I not mow it at all?

A: Read our lips: DO NOT cut your grass short. The length you have been leaving all summer to shade the ground will insulate the roots. Unless we have a very unusual winter, you won't have consistent snow cover to protect your lawn's roots.

(Do not base your expectations of what this winter will be like on what happened last year. We mention this for the benefit of relative newcomers to Montana. Those who have been around a while already know better.)

It won't hurt to leave your lawn unmowed, but it will make it messier in the spring. We recommend mowing it to the proper height – two and a half to three inches. If you haven't been doing that all along, here's your last chance to redeem yourself.

Q: Do I keep putting things in my compost pile, now that it is getting so cold?

A: Yes. The worst that can happen is that they will rot very slowly. If you don't put things in there, they won't do you any good at all. Do you want all those goodies to be relegated to the landfill?

One of the good things about our winters' wild temperature swings is that it gets warm enough to rot things some days.

We have no evidence, but we suspect that we get more compost made in the winter than other areas do because of this – plus the fact that we don't get constant snow cover to insulate the pile against the temperature changes.

We turn our compost twice a year, once in October and again in April or May. Often we are amazed at how much good compost has formed during the winter.

Some scientific work has been done on winter composting. Studies at Cornell University suggest three things to help in this endeavor: wrap the south side of the pile with black plastic to get full benefit whenever the sun does come out; cover the pile with a blanket or thick layer of straw to help hold the heat; and make the pile bigger than usual in winter to increase the core temperature.

Most of what we put in the compost in winter is kitchen garbage. When we go to dump it, we add water and take it out sloppy wet. We don't get enough snow in this area to keep the compost wet enough to decompose. We have never had a compost barrel get too wet.

The temperature range at which composting happens is broader than some purists think. Nor does it really matter if you have the exact proportions of green and brown materials in your pile. We have seen several very specific recipes, no two of which are alike. We believe that a laissez faire attitude is a good one.

At this time of year we have a lot of dead leaves. But if you rake them all up at once and put them in the compost, they make a very effective watershed, like a tin roof. The precipitation hits the leaves and runs off down the sides, leaving the rest of the organic material to dry out. You can water a pile of leaves all winter long and not have one drop stay in the pile.

It is better to put in a few inches of leaves and store the rest to add after putting in a good layer of kitchen garbage. If you feel you must get all the leaves in there on the same day, layer them with garden soil. It also is advisable to throw in a handful of starter – nitrogen – a little more often in winter to encourage all those good bugs to work in the cold.

Q: My grandma's Christmas cactus always bloomed beautifully for her — why won't mine do the same for me?

Q: My Christmas cactus gets buds all over it, but before they open, they dry up and fall off – what's the problem?

Q: I have tried everything to get this Christmas cactus to bloom, but I have yet to see a flower. Is there any hope?

A: Late September, and 'tis the season for Christmas cactus questions. The most important thing for any Christmas cactus keeper to remember is that it is a short-day plant.

Actually, it is a long-night plant. But when they discovered that years ago, they didn't realize it was the dark the plant cared about.

If the days are longer than the nights, a Christmas cactus makes green stuff. If the nights are longer than the days, it makes flower buds. It is somewhat temperature-sensitive, too, preferring a little cool with its dark.

Try to see that your cactus gets little or no artificial light at this time of year. The next two months are the time that matters if you want it to bloom around Christmas.

It doesn't require absolute dark, as poinsettias do. If the light is too dim for you to read, it is OK for a Christmas cactus. If you move it into a dimmer room, be sure it gets good light in the daytime.

Even when it is getting more darkness it will probably be a month before you will notice anything happening. Don't fret – it's working on some flowers.

The closer your plant is, genetically, to your grandma's, the more likely it is to bloom. The newer ones are more highly refined, bred for large flowers and different colors. Yellow is the current rage. They are not meant to rebloom. They are over-bred and too refined. If your neighbor's plant blooms and yours doesn't, it may just be the kinds of plants with which you started.

Let your plant dry out a little. It's a succulent, so that's not too dangerous.

Christmas cacti have small root systems and don't like to be over-potted – to have a pot with more room than they need. In comparison to other houseplants, they have a lot more upstairs than downstairs.

If you have a huge plant, it may not bloom as well as one that has been pruned. Remember this for next year, but it's too late to prune now.

You would just cut off any flower buds it might have in store.

If your plant blooms, but not profusely or beautifully, prune the heck out of it and next year it will repay you. Some Christmas cactus plants will bloom again in the spring. Some, once in bloom, stay at it for up to three months.

Dropping buds are probably caused by bright evening light in the time before most of the buds are open. If you lengthen its day when the buds are small, it will drop them all and go back into the leaf-making mode. It is normal, however, for it to drop a few of its buds.

Q: *My fall-blooming asters have been lovely, but they are finished now. Is it safe to cut them down?*

A: Yes. Any perennial can be cut down as soon as it gets brown and ugly. It probably won't kill it to do so sooner, but it is best to give the plant a chance to reverse its plumbing system and flush the nutrients from the leaves back down to the roots. That gives the plants a boost in the spring.

Fall asters are mostly the New England wildflower also called Michaelmas daisies. They bloom after everything else is through, with the possible exceptions of pansies and primroses. They will bloom even after a freeze that puts many perennials to sleep for the winter. They are unfazed by temperatures in the low 20s.

The wildflowers are lavender in color and tall, but there now are a lot of garden cultivars, as well. A couple of our favorites are a deep raspberry variety called Alma Potschke and a short dark violet one named Purple Dome.

New England asters are three to four feet tall and have ugly legs. One of the nice things about the short sort is that you can plant them in front of the tall ones. Of course you can plant other things in front too, as long as they have nice foliage to hide several inches of dead leaves and brown stems.

Q: Do I need to dig up my glads this fall? My neighbor didn't dig hers last year and they did fine. If I do need to, is it too late to do it now?

A: Perhaps your neighbor has some of the "hardy gladiolus" now on the market. They are marginally hardy here, but your neighbor probably was darned lucky last winter, and their survival is unlikely two years in a row. The corms are tough, but they won't tolerate freezing.

It's not too late to dig yours until they freeze, which doesn't happen for weeks after the tops are frosted. Even if everything above ground is frozen, the ground itself is not.

After digging the glads, cut the tops off and store the corms in a paper bag in a dry, cool place. They tolerate quite a wide range of temperatures.

It's probably too late now, but next spring if you haven't kept track of which color is which, you'll wish you had. In any gladiolus garden, there will be one that out-performs all the others, and after two years you will be trying to give away the progeny of the top producers. Some judicious birth control can prevent that problem.

Q: I dug my dahlia tubers and set them out to dry, but they are already starting to shrivel up. What should I have done?

A: Dahlias are trickier to care for than glads and much pickier about temperature. They can't stand to get close to freezing and would rather be at 50 degrees than 30.

There are a lot of pet methods for storing dahlias, but one that works for us is to put them in a paper bag, bury it in peat moss, and store it on a high shelf in a cool room where the glad corms are stored on the floor. Then every month or so give them just a sprinkle of water. Dahlias need to be dry or they'll rot, but in this climate, if they get no moisture, many will have just dried out and died by planting time.

Another method is to store the tuber in a pot of dirt. The dirt should be kept fairly dry all winter, but just short of turning to dust.

When you dig the dahlias, they look like bouquets of sweet potatoes attached to a central stem. It's easier to leave the fingers attached until spring. Whenever you separate them, you must leave a little piece of the stem, or neck, attached to each tuber or it will not grow, period.

Q: I have been given some columbine seed. Can I plant it now? If I don't what should I do with it?

A: Yes, you certainly can plant it now. Some columbines do better for exposure to winter cold and it shouldn't hurt any of them to spend a winter in your garden.

Scatter the seed and just barely cover it. Some columbine seeds will germinate better with light. If you choose a place out of the wind, you can merely press the little seeds into the soil. Put a stake by each patch you sow. You might think you'll remember in the spring exactly where you put them, but if our experience is any indication, you won't.

If for some reason you don't want to plant them now, they should be stored in a dry, cool place. It's also fine to put them in an airtight container in the freezer. Then plant them in the same way in the very early spring. (You may think the weather will be nicer then, but you'll probably be wrong about that, too.)

If you really want to fuss with your columbine seeds, plant them in a pot, moisten everything and give it a month in the refrigerator. What all of these methods provide is cold stratification.

Q: The peonies I ordered came a couple of weeks ago but I haven't got them planted. Can I plant them now? If not, how should I keep them over the winter?

A: Yes, plant your peonies now. The buds for next year's growth are already formed, so it won't hurt if they don't have time to develop much of a root system before freeze-up.

One year, Molly ordered some from a peony specialty nursery in Minnesota. Bad weather prevented the company from digging and shipping until very late in the fall. They arrived in mid-November and she planted them, although it was an arduous and unpleasant job. All of them flourished.

Do give the newcomers a thick comforter of mulch so that when we get those few weird, warm, sunny days in February or March the peonies don't wake up prematurely.

Q: My delphinium finished blooming long ago, but there were delphinium in arrangements at the fair. How did those people get their delphinium to bloom at this time of the year?

A: Your delphiniums are the perennial ones. Those blooming now are the annual variety, sometimes called larkspur, especially in their single forms. Double forms are more likely to be called delphinium. The botanical name on the seed packet may be *Delphinium* something, but it also could be *Consolida* something or other. They are the same thing, whichever it says. If you're looking in seed catalogs, choose something called annual delphinium.

Q: I have some blackberry plants I got from some old plants a few miles away from here. They grew well the first year, but this year didn't grow as much and had very few berries on them. I use organic fertilizer. Do blackberries need some special nutrients in the soil? Do they require extra water?

A: First of all, blackberries are marginal in this climate. That means if you grow them in a protected spot they will do fine and you'll say, "Blackberries are easy." But if you put them in an exposed area, you will ask, "What's wrong with my blackberries?"

It is quite typical here to get winter damage on the first-year canes. Blackberry canes, like other brambles, grow two years, making leaves the first year and both leaves and berries the next. Winter damage causes die-back in the canes and poor fruiting.

We suggest you look at the growing conditions of your bushes' parent plants. Do they have some sort of protection? You are likely to find they are in a spot protected from northwest and west winds. Try to duplicate these conditions in your own patch. You may need to move them to a place sheltered by buildings, shrubs or trees upwind. (We are only talking about winter wind – the bushes won't be hurt by summer weather.)

If you can't or don't want to move them, consider putting up a wind break. You can use a fence – about 50 percent solid wood, so that half the wind comes through – just west of the bushes. For a real quick fix, you can buy the green netting made just for wind protection. It is light weight and requires no major construction to hold it up. You might also try mulching the blackberries heavily for the winter.

Your organic fertilizer should be fine. Blackberries don't need anything your other plants don't need. They do require irrigation, but no more than the rest of the garden.

If you want to keep these plants going while you start some in a more sheltered area, it is easily done. Bend a cane down and throw a shovelful of dirt on it about six inches from the end, burying the cane and leaving the top sticking out. During the growing season the cane will root under that shovelful of dirt. Once it is growing, cut off the old cane, dig the new plant and move it to the more protected location. You can sometimes speed up the rooting by scraping the bottom side of the cane where it will be buried.

You didn't ask about planting them, but we will tell you anyway, not to make the mistake of planting a double row of blackberries. Even if you think you have allowed plenty of room between the rows, odds are, that you haven't. On a hot summer day, it is no fun to try to go between two rows of blackberries to pick the fruit only to get scratched to death. And it also is no fun to have to pick your blackberries on a hot summer day while wearing a heavy jacket for protection. (Do you get the idea that we have been there ourselves?) There is no such thing as a "thornless" blackberry. Thornless blackberries just have shorter thorns. They don't call these plants brambles for nothing.

Q: My fern-leafed, satiny-red peony produced seed this year, which I saved by collecting in little bags. At $25 per plant, which I saw in a catalog, I have about 100 potential plants. Do you know how I should treat the seed? Stratify in the refrigerator? How long? Plant now? How deep?

A: Let nature do the chilling for you. Plant them in any kind of small flower pot while the seed is still fresh and bury the pot almost up to the rim in an outdoor flower bed where you will be able to keep track of it for quite a long time. Next year you won't see anything. Peonies belong to the group of plants that put out a root before putting up any leaves, which is what they will do in their first year before going dormant for the winter.

The following year you will see your first leaf.

If you don't want to wait that long, you can hurry the process a little bit. It is done indoors. With a sharp knife or rasp, make a hole through the seed coat to admit water more readily. Plant your seeds in a plastic bag with a little bit of seed-starting soil – you are going to have to watch them. Leave at room temperature someplace out of direct sunlight (which would cook them in their plastic bag) and they should start germinating in two or three months. After eight months have passed, every seed that is going to grow a root will have done it.

The root will get a few inches long. Check every couple of weeks, take out the ones that have a nice root, put each one of them in its own little pot and put the pots in a plastic bag in the refrigerator.

Check them regularly. After two or three months, the leaves should begin to show. When that happens, bring the plants back up to house temperature and plant them outdoors as soon as the weather is warm enough. That way you have essentially condensed two years' worth of growth into one year.

The reason it takes so long is probably because the peony seed is immature and has to continue developing before it can germinate.

In addition, it will be at least five or six years before the plants will begin to bloom.

You might have quite a bit of fun doing this, but the resulting flowers are not going to look like their mom. There is no longer any such thing as a species peony. Peonies have been cultivated and hybridized for hundreds of years, probably starting with the Chinese. By now, what we have is hybrids of hybrids of hybrids. You might get a wonderful plant, but the chances are greater that you will get something fairly uninteresting.

Five years is a long time to wait to see if your efforts have been worth it. If what you want is more fern-leafed, satiny-red peonies, it would be easier and faster to propagate the one you have by root divisions. If you decide to start with your seeds, do it for the trip and not the destination.

Q: I am digging potatoes and have discovered terrible problems from wireworms. Is there anything to be done about them?

A: There are things you can do, but that does NOT include spraying any kind of insecticide because nothing will get them. It helps to know that the wireworm is the larva of a click beetle, which quits eating your potatoes once it grows out of its hungry, teen-age stage. Click beetles like grassy areas and wireworms usually cause the most problems next to grass or in areas just plowed up from grass.

If you can be patient and plant something other than potatoes in that area for a couple of years, the wireworms will have disappeared by the time you plant potatoes there again.

Wireworms are not a pest that occurs in thousands, so you can cut down their numbers by watching for them and killing individuals. They live in the top few inches of soil, so you find them when cultivating, planting or weeding – anything that moves a little earth around. It's not as bad as it sounds – you are not going to be grubbing around in the subterranean depths looking for a creature. They are highly visible – orange, between 1 and 2 inches in length, and looking like a legless centipede. They move fast, with a sidewinder motion. You really can catch them.

The third prong of wireworm eradication is trapping. As bait you use their favorite foods – potatoes – or alternatively, carrots. Cut a potato, bury big chunks about an inch deep and check on them every couple of days. If you have wireworms, and you hold your mouth right and the garden gods smile upon you, every time you dig one up, you will find a wireworm. Unless you are really unlucky, they will not be throughout your garden, but only in one spot. You will be able to plant other things there until the worms move on.

Q: We have our place up for sale and I want to divide a favorite wild Alaskan rose bush so I can take some with me. Is this a time to do it?

A: A hardy wild rose on its own roots is much easier to propagate than a grafted hybrid tea. Although we prefer spring, this is an acceptable time to move perennials. With a plant you are attached to, we recommend doing two divisions, just in case everything doesn't go as planned. Try to get a medium-sized chunk – you want some good roots and not too much top for those roots to support. Do not try to prune the top to match the size to the roots. Let the plant prune itself, which it will do. It knows which branches are connected to its remaining roots and you do not. It is very easy to cut off the wrong canes by mistake.

Since you don't yet have the spot where the division will eventually live, put it in a pot the roots will fit into easily. It just needs enough room to grow little feeder roots. You don't want a whole lot of unoccupied soil in there: that situation is an invitation to dampness and root rot. Dig a big hole and line it with some loose insulation like pine needles or straw and "plant" the pot. The insulation will keep the roots from freezing and make the pot easy to dig up when the ground is frozen. At freeze-up, give it a healthy mulch of pine needles or straw and just leave it there, or take it into the cellar or some other cold place. Outside is best – it must remain dormant.

Keep the soil moist, but not wet. You don't want it to dehydrate, but you don't want it to grow, either.

If you want to hedge your bets, you can also take some cuttings and plant some seeds.

Make your cuttings after the leaves drop. Have some containers filled with potting soil. Using a knife (scissors crush the cane ends) cut sections of canes a 1/4 to 1-inch in diameter and about 6 inches long, taking them from this year's growth. Cut just below where a leaf had grown, and when you plant them in the pots, be sure you know you have the bottom of the stem in the soil and not the top.

Plant the pots in insulated holes, as described above. Cover them with mulch or row covers so they don't dehydrate.

Or you can put your cuttings in damp peat moss or vermiculite, wrap them up and store them in the cellar. However you do it, take plenty of cuttings because not all of them are going to grow.

To start from scratch, take some seeds from your rose hips when they ripen – putting them in a little water and fermenting the seeds out is as easy a way as any. Put all the seeds you get into a three- or four-inch pot with potting soil and put the pot outside in a sheltered place.

Be prepared to wait a while. Some may germinate next summer, but some may take two or three years. Don't give up on them for a long, long time. Just keep track of the pot, protect it from the worst winter weather while you are waiting and don't let it dry out.

Q: I am overwhelmed with a plant that I think is called wild morning glory. I can't get rid of it. I have pulled it and sprayed it and dug it up. What do I do?

A: This plant is also called bindweed. Lucky gardeners don't have any. You're not one of them. You can recognize it as a vine with heart-shaped leaves and white or pink flowers.

It is very difficult to get rid of. Hang in there. Keep trying. It will take a few years, but eventually you will get rid of it unless someone directly upwind from you has a plantation of it that keeps blowing seed into your yard.

Just keep cutting it off. You can pull – it won't hurt to jerk the plant you see, but don't dig it. That just encourages bindweed. It reproduces from root cuttings, so every time you cut in with a spade you have made a bunch of root cuttings that will reproduce. It is very unlikely you could ever get the whole root because it is capable of going ten feet deep; even with power equipment, you would miss some and you would have ruined your whole garden in the process.

If you just keep cutting the foliage to ground level, the roots will eventually die. You don't have to remove the vine, just separate the plant from its roots. The roots will put up shoots again, but they can't survive if you don't let them make leaves.

TRY TO KEEP IT FROM GOING TO SEED! When you start seeing the morning glory flowers, be doubly vigilant.

Q: This year I got a bleeding heart and it bloomed beautifully, but early in August it started turning yellow and eventually it all died. I want to plant more next year, but don't want them to die, too. Do I need to plant them in a different location? What are bleeding heart's special requirements?

A: Yours obviously is the big bleeding heart because that is the one that blooms once and then goes dormant. It's not dead, it's just dozing. There is a small bleeding heart that blooms all summer long and does not go dormant until after frost.

The big, old-fashioned bleeding heart blooms in the spring and goes dormant in summer when other things are flourishing. If your plant did fine this year, it probably will do a repeat performance next spring. Don't compost this year's plant. We recommend that you mulch it, though, since this will be its first winter.

Bleeding hearts require part-day sun, and it is a good idea not to put them against a south-facing wall where they will sprout early in the spring and have their flower buds killed by late frosts.

Q: I have a willow tree that is now too big for its space and it needs drastic pruning. Is it OK to prune a willow, and if so, is this a good time?

Q: I have some overgrown junipers that have been trimmed before, but need it again. Can I do that now?

A: This is really not a good time to prune anything. You can cut off dead stuff or diseased portions anytime, but from late July on, one shouldn't prune any woody plants until they are well into dormancy.

As we have said many a time, pruning stimulates growth, encouraging the plant to make new twigs. There isn't enough of the season left for the new growth to mature and harden before the first really cold weather kills it. This probably wouldn't kill the tree, but you are assured that at least some of the new growth will die.

You will have to trim those dead portions off in the spring anyway, so you might as well wait until spring and just prune once.

The willow, like all deciduous trees, is best pruned while deep in dormancy – in the vicinity of February. It is possible to do some light pruning in early summer just to control size. That does have a dwarfing effect.

The junipers are like all conifers in that you can prune them over a longer stretch of the year, although dormant pruning is best.

To encourage dwarfing in conifers, wait until their new spring growth is done (you will have a lot of light green tips) and then cut off or break off most of that.

Pruning for dwarfing just slows down a plant's growth – you can't turn a giant specimen into a miniature.

Q: I have a row of Arctic willows that have grown bigger than I expected. I have to cut them way back. When should I do that?

Q: We have a climbing honeysuckle we want to put on a trellis next spring, but for now it is climbing all over the ground. We are sure we can cut it back without hurting it, but when should we do it?

A: The best time for both is when they are deep in dormancy. Dormancy is not something that happens the minute the leaves fall off and ends when the buds swell next spring. It is like a very slow falling asleep and leisurely waking up. It is a good idea to wait until January or February, when the plants are really sound asleep, before doing any pruning. All the cuts will heal fastest then and that is when the open cuts will be least likely to be attacked by diseases.

Right now is a really bad time to prune anything. The plants are starting to rest, but are easily confused into thinking they should start to grow again. Pruning a plant is an overt order to a plant, "GROW." If you say it in October, the plant tries to follow orders instead of going to sleep. If you wait to say it in January it will say, "OK, as soon as it is spring, I will," and nod off for the winter.

Concerning the Arctic willows, plants that get too big for their places always are a problem. If you don't want to move them to a place with more elbowroom, the best solution probably is to prune them drastically – about six inches tall. You are likely to have to keep doing that about every six years.

With the honeysuckle, you can make a trellis a winter project. Tie the honeysuckle up to it any time before it starts to grow again (the honeysuckle, not the trellis), trim it to the shape you want and clip off any branches you broke in the process. It won't hurt the plant to cut everything off to twelve to eighteen inches, but you might as well salvage any long pieces you can.

Any pruning should be done when the temperature is comfortable enough to be out there. Comfortable is a personal sort of thing, but the magic number is 19 degrees. Don't prune when it is very cold.

Q: I have three monarda bushes two years old. Last year they grew but didn't bloom. This year they bloomed very well, but now they're dying back. Is this their normal pattern?

A: Yes, it would not be surprising for this to happen, although you can usually keep the foliage green longer if you deadhead the plants – cut the blossoms off as they fade.

Remember that the hot days of late summer are stressful for perennials. Are you giving them plenty of water to help counteract the hot weather? Be sure it isn't powdery mildew that is causing the leaf problems; you may want to treat the mildew if it exists.

You probably already know not to fertilize any perennial at this time of year – wait for early spring to do that.

Q: I have been growing cucumbers for years and this year for the first time have bitter cucumbers. What's wrong? Somebody told me to cut the ends off and the middle would be fine. That was true for some of them, but others were bitter all the way through. What causes this?

A: You can blame it on A) the weather or B) genetics – maybe both.

Bitterness comes from having the soil moisture fluctuate, and the plant has to get dry only once for the cucumbers developing at that time to turn bitter. Fortunately, that doesn't apply to any cucumbers that had not yet started to develop. So if you kept the soil moist after that, the later cucumbers should be all right.

The other piece of the answer is that some cucumbers have been bred without the gene that produces bitterness. If you order your seed from a catalog you might want to look next year for ones that can't get bitter. Those are usually the very thin skinned ones that you don't have to peel, an added bonus.

Q: My tuberous begonias are six or seven years old. I treat them exactly the same way every year, except that I repotted them in fresh dirt a year and a half ago. They are in six-inch pots. This year they didn't do much. The flowers were fewer and smaller. One pot didn't bloom at all. Are they just so old that they need to be thrown away?

A: They really shouldn't be senile yet, and may just resent the reduction in their living area. They aren't ready for a nursing home room after having been accustomed to a nice big apartment. Tuberous begonias are not among the plants that bloom best when they are root bound. A six-inch pot would be adequate for a small, young tuber, but by now yours must need at least an eight-inch pot and a ten- or twelve-inch one wouldn't hurt if the tuber is large.

Since they had been doing fine for you, we assume that you are treating them well and don't need to change anything else but their living quarters. Why don't you wait until spring when you are ready to restart them to repot them again. It won't hurt to winter them in the small pots.

While you are repotting them, check their depth. They also don't like to be too deep – the tops should be just barely covered. There is even an argument about that, with some people saying the tubers should be on the surface. We prefer to have them covered because then roots can grow out of the top as well as the bottom, but they certainly don't like to be too deep. Even though you will be adding some fresh soil next spring, keep on fertilizing. Begonias like a little snack about once a month during the growing season.

Q: What can I do about all these terrible box elder bugs? They're crawling up my walls – I find them everywhere. I tried spraying with diazinon, but it didn't help. I tried swatting, but that's labor intensive and they smell bad when you squash them. I've asked everybody I know and they just told me to call Dirty Fingernails.

A: We wish Dirty Fingernails could give you an easy answer, but there isn't one. You won't get rid of the bugs as long as you have a female box elder tree. Diazinon and other insecticides are ineffective because the bugs are not feeding – they are just looking for a place to overwinter.

It is best to try to remove them, rather than kill them. Sweep them up, tie them in a plastic bag and take them far, far away. For a permanent solution, you are going to have to cut down that tree.

Box elder bugs are worse some years than others and they are much more of a problem east of the divide than west because they have so many more box elder trees east of the Rockies.

For any readers who don't know if they have one or not, the box elder also is called an ash-leaved maple. It's one of the really tough prairie trees.

A gardener tells us that wasp and hornet spray will kill box elder bugs – not just the one on which she scores a direct hit, but also those that come along later and walk where she sprayed. We haven't tried this, but having suffered through box elder bug invasions, we can understand her willingness to try anything and everything. She didn't say what it did to her wallpaper.

Q: I have a really good crop of large carrots this year, but so many of them are splitting. What causes this? Do they need more acid soil?

A: You must have taken very good care of your carrots, thinning them well and tending them carefully to get such nice big ones. The problem may be simply one of their age. When carrots are left in the ground after they pass the peak of maturity, they do split. For right now, all you can do is to pull those that haven't split, before they do. Harvest the split ones and eat them first – they won't store well.

Another cause of the problem is fluctuation in soil moisture during the growing period. When the carrots are in fairly dry soil and you give them a big drink, the root takes up the water faster than the outside of the carrot can cope with it and it splits. To prevent that next time, give your carrots a drink before they get too dry. Also, be sure that the soil in which you plant them has plenty of organic matter to hold water longer and help equalize the moisture supply.

Next year consider planting some of your crop in May for eating during the growing season and some in June to provide more for storage. Or just plant all of them later than you did this year. They will grow fine in the cool weather of the spring, but most carrots that grow well around here mature before the end of the warm weather.

Q: Would you write about roses? I need to know everything because I don't know anything.

A: We can offer some interesting tidbits, but not everything there is to say about roses. There is no end to the things that can be said about roses.

This is the time people begin thinking about mulching roses for winter. There are two systems – one for hardy roses and another for hybrid teas.

You treat hardy roses just like any perennial – in their first fall give them three or four inches of anything organic and loose. The mulch must be loose enough to have air spaces. In following years, when their roots are deeper, they need no winter protection. Someone recently asked if her nice, composted manure would make a good mulch for roses, but it wouldn't. It is a good summer mulch when you want to feed them but not a good winter mulch when you want to ventilate them.

There are almost as many ways of mulching tea roses as there are tea rose growers. The main thing is to make sure the graft – that lump just below where the bush begins to branch – is very well protected. We like to mound at least three inches of soil over the graft. Then we set a wire cage, three feet tall and about a foot wider than the bush, around it and fill the cage with mulch.

Remember, winter mulch is not there to keep your roses warm. Its purpose is to keep them cold. In this climate the problem is not the cold – roses are dormant in the winter anyway. What you are trying to protect them from is the warm days in February that fool them into believing it's May and breaking dormancy just in time for our next siege of 20 below. Mulch shades the ground so it will stay frozen on those balmy midwinter days.

You don't want to put your mulch on until after Thanksgiving. (Yes, this does mean that if you have already mulched your roses you must take the mulch off again, temporarily.)

A gardener asked us about a hybrid tea rose that this year grew one branch with its usual, lovely blossoms and another that never bloomed at all, although it grew very tall and leafy. That is what you get when your hybrid tea is damaged above the graft. The good part was grafted on, and the bloomless part is coming from the hardy root to which it was grafted. It is more common to have the entire graft die and leave only the hardy root stock, which is likely to resemble a wild rose.

In the spring, with hybrid teas you wait until they start leafing out in the middle of the mulch before removing it. You may end up leaving mulch on until May or June, when we usually get that one last, hard frost.

One advantage to the hardy roses is that if the bush is damaged in that last frost, all you need to do is prune off the damaged portion. It will come back very quickly. If it freezes all the way to the ground, it will come up from the roots and produce blossoms just like you had last year. Grafted roses that freeze to the ground and come up from the roots can't bloom like the part above the graft. It died.

The hybrid teas and floribundas are both upright plants and have fairly stiff canes. They are the kind you most often see in formal rose gardens. A basic difference between them is the way they bloom. Hybrid teas have large flowers with long stems. Floribundas bear clusters of smaller blossoms. Both are capable of blooming almost nonstop for up to six months in a climate with that much weather above freezing, and they do go for a long time here.

One of the disadvantages of hybrid teas is that they get diseases easily because of the extensive breeding they have gone through to get the large flowers. We recently read about a rosarian in Connecticut who solved his problem of hardiness in his hybrid teas by treating them as annuals. You might be able to afford that if you don't want 100 bushes in your yard at all times.

If you are growing the old-fashioned roses, the ones often called antique roses, you needn't worry about disease at all because all the old ones that were susceptible to diseases have died of them. The modern descendants, generally called hardy roses, are not entirely disease proof, but very close. Most growers of hardy roses recommend that you plan not to spray them (the bushes, not the growers).

The term hardy roses covers several different species. Some may be crosses of two species. One common line is rugosa, which offers reblooming so you don't get one huge flowering season in the spring and a bloomless bush all summer long – like Austrian Copper or Persian Yellow, which are foetida, rather than rugosa. Rugosa parentage also offers scent, the old-fashioned rose smell you used to love in your grandmother's garden.

The modern hardy roses range in size from ground covers to climbers. More, however, are in the category called shrub roses, which mature between three and six feet and tend to be about as wide as they are tall. Their biggest drawback is that they do not make good cut flowers.

If you have been reading about David Austin's English roses, those would be worth trying if you are in a sheltered spot and consider yourself Zone 5. If you are in an unsheltered Zone 4, don't bother.

Miniature roses are a separate variety. Some are as hardy as the so-called hardy roses. If you ever want to see a class of roses with 1,000 new names a year, look at the miniatures. Like hardy roses, they are not grafted. You want to put them in pots, in a small bed or in the front of a larger bed so they will not be out of scale with their neighbors. These days they range from micro-minis to plants about eighteen inches in height, twice the size of what you expect a miniature to be. (Are they macro-minis?) The miniatures bloom all during the growing season; they have a flush of bloom about every six weeks and make excellent cut flowers.

As far as we know there is no list of which are the hardiest, so about all you can do is try them and see which ones survive. They cost only about half as much as a hybrid tea, so it may be twice as easy to treat them as annuals.

Climbing roses are not really climbers because they have nothing to hang on with. They have long shoots that require support. If you want them to go up a wall or trellis, you must fasten them on. Keep tying in the shoots so they grow the way you want them to. ("Train them up in the way they should grow and when they are old, they will not depart from it.") As with children, you must do the training during the growing season when the canes are still flexible.

For the maximum number of flowers, try to keep the shoots as horizontal as possible. If you are growing them up a rose pillar, for instance, train them around and around, rather than straight up. If you don't want to tie them in, you can train them to go up a tree or even a shrub. It is really a beautiful sight to see a climbing rose blooming in the middle of something else. Just plant it at least six feet away from the trunk, because if you plant it closer, it won't get enough water. You can use a pole or a cord of some kind to train it up until it gets to the first tree branch. After that, its thorns will hook it in. If it is to climb a shrub, pick a rose that's not going to get big enough to pull down the shrub.

Q: I have a larch tree that keeps getting a fungus disease. I keep spraying it and it still gets it. What can I do?

Q: Some of my raspberry leaves are all brown and look skeletonized. I have checked them over and there are no visible bugs. What could be doing this?

Q: My delphinium died and I wonder if it got rust from the hollyhocks that were growing behind it.

Q: Some of my strawberry leaves have turned brown but I can't find any creatures. What's wrong with them?

A: All of these problems have to do with fungi, but they are not all the same disease. For all practical purposes it doesn't matter because most of the things you do to combat fungi are the same no matter which one is causing the problem.

Notice that we did not say "treat a fungus." Once the disease is there, you are not going to get rid of it entirely and all you can do is damage control. Most fungicides are preventives and in order to treat a fungus with most of the commercially available fungicide sprays, you must spray a couple of weeks before the disease becomes visible. You must keep spraying, usually at weekly intervals, for as long as you think the disease is going to be around to attack the plant. Very time consuming, very boring, very expensive. Unless you are someone like a commercial grower who makes a science of keeping track of all the variables from year to year, the fungus probably will get there first. In our gardens the fungus usually wins the race. This explains why no matter how often you spray your larch tree you haven't got rid of the disease. We know of only a couple of sprays that can be applied once the fungus disease is visible and which offer much hope that it will kill at least part of a fungal colony.

One product is so common and so benign that it lives in your kitchen cabinet with the parsley flakes and spends its declining years in the back of your refrigerator. It's baking soda. You know that is not a miracle cure, because the Japanese and English have been using it on fungus diseases for a few centuries now and still are using it today. If it were not at least partially effective they would have given up the practice long ago, but if it were totally successful, the fungal diseases would have been eliminated from their part of the world.

Another product is a fairly new extract of neem oil called by different trade names by different manufacturers. Our experience with it has been good. We haven't used it long enough or on enough kinds of plants to know how good it's going to be. We are pretty sure it won't be a miracle either.

A third benign fungicide is cinnamon. Sprinkled on as a powder or sprayed as a modified cinnamon oil, it looks like another weapon in the anti-fungal wars. The modified oil extract must be purchased; plain oil of cinnamon kills leaves when they are exposed to sunlight.

What can you do? The main thing is to get rid of all the fungal spores you can and to eliminate the places such spores can overwinter and gather forces to attack your plants in the spring. And you can position and prune your plants to make them less vulnerable.

When a fungus disease is active, like when your rose buds suddenly get bright orange lumps or the bottom leaves of your hollyhocks get spots, cut off all the infected parts and don't drop them on the ground under the plant. Many fungal diseases are specific to a particular plant, so you don't have to rush for the nearest air-tight container to hold the debris, but it does make sense that you don't leave the rose rust spores on the ground near a rose plant. Even though it breaks your heart to cut off the infected bud, you must do it because it is never going to open anyway. You could think of it as an emergency amputation or partial vegetative euthanasia. Hoping the disease will go away only contributes to its spread.

At the end of the season clean up all the dead leaves and other plant debris under any plant that had a fungus disease this year. Wherever you choose to dispose of the infected debris, don't put it upwind from the vulnerable plants and don't put it in your compost pile unless you know yours is a hot pile. Once you have cleaned up the ground thoroughly, some spores will still be left on the soil surface. Cover them up with a layer of compost mulch so that in the spring the spores can't get through to attack the new sprouts. Your next line of defense is a garden diary. Keep a watchful eye on the current year's plants and note in the book anything you need to watch for next year as your plants develop.

How can you tell if what your plant has is a fungal disease? By the time you can say "The leaves have turned brown," or "The plant died without any apparent insect attack," all you can do is assume that it was a fungus disease. After all, 80 percent of plant diseases are caused by fungus. All fungal diseases end up with the same product – brown leaves or a dead plant. With perennial plants, usually the whole plant is not dead, only this year's growth, so the delphinium will be back.

When that delphinium comes up (or any other plant vulnerable to fungal disease) give it the best possible air circulation. Fungi do not thrive in moving air. Usually that means thinning and pruning. As the season progresses and the growth in the beds gets thicker, keep cutting out the weak stems. Sometimes when you do a good job thinning it is all the fungus-fighting you will have to do.

Q: Is it right that I should plant my garlic in the fall?

A: Yes, you plant garlic in the fall because that will give you the biggest bulbs. You will get a crop if you plant in the spring, but they won't be as big. Plant garlic as soon as the weather cools down. You want the plants to grow several inches of root but no tops before the ground freezes.

There are basically two types of garlic: hard neck and soft neck. There also is elephant garlic, which is not truly garlic but a member of the leek family. Of the true garlics, there are at least 300 cultivated varieties. The hard-neck garlics have a stiff stem and are the more primitive type. They have a greater range of flavor and are easier to peel. The soft-neck garlics are the kind you see in the grocery store. They are bigger and hotter, have more garlicky flavor and store better. Whichever kind you decide to plant, choose the biggest cloves in a head to plant and eat the small ones. The big cloves will produce bigger heads. Put them where you can get water to them but where the drainage is good. Plant the cloves four to five inches apart and about an inch deep. That's all you need to do now, except to make sure the soil stays moist. Don't forget to mulch them when the ground freezes, at Thanksgiving time or later.

If you forget to mulch, you still will have some garlic next year, but some probably will have died from the cold. Take the mulch off in the spring when the plants start to come up, probably in late March. You needn't do anything all summer but keep them weeded and watered. Harvest the garlic at the end of the summer when you see that the leaves have turned brown. If you have grown the hard-neck garlics, they will develop what looks like flower buds at the top of the stalk but actually are tiny little bulbs. If you are trying to multiply your garlic, save those bulblets and plant them. Otherwise, cut the stalk off to allow all the plant's strength to go to the cloves developing underground.

After you have dug the garlic bulbs, dry them with the tops on at something like room temperature. After everything is dry, you can break off the dirt and tops and some of the outer skin, but leave a layer or two of the papery stuff. Store them in a dry place in an airy container like a net produce bag or the leg of nylon panty hose. If you are feeling fancy, you can make a garlic braid, although you must do that before the leaves have entirely dried out. You won't know how good your varieties are until they have been stored about a month – that's when the flavor is at its peak.

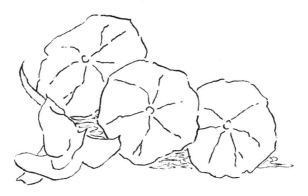

Q: When should I cut down my perennials?

A; We believe in applying the rule of aesthetics: Leave them there until they look bad and then compost them. That means that we have been cutting ours down here and there for the past two months. There are some we won't chop off for another two months.

Aside from the way they look, the main reason for cutting them back is so you don't start next year with a bunch of fungal diseases in your flowerbeds waiting to attack the new growth. The bad fungi that live in the beds are more of a problem in warm, humid climates than in our cool, dry one.

If you have plants like grasses that look attractive all winter, there is no reason not to leave them all winter. If you have plants that are semi-evergreen, like perennial candytuft or wild ginger, there is no reason to cut them back until the leaves start looking ugly, which may be in February. Some other perennials' leaves look terrible after the first frost, and those are the first ones to get rid of.

If you are a neatnik and want everything in all your beds trimmed and tidy in the fall, cutting everything then won't do too much damage, but any plant whose leaves are still green is still making sugars and transporting them to the roots for storage. When you cut off green leaves, you cut off part of next year's food supply.

Another consideration is protection of the crowns and roots in bad weather. When the top of the plant is there, even dead, it is making a windbreak or shelter for the crown. Once you cut all the tops down – usually to about an inch and a half – it also is a good idea to add a layer of mulch or compost to conserve soil moisture. Perhaps most importantly, when weed seeds blow in, the mulch denies them a place to root.

If you go south for the winter and don't cut your perennials down, or just never get around to it, the only thing really important is to get them cut off before the old stems get mixed up with the new growth next spring. The plants most likely to cause this problem are columbines and iris. One icy March day trying to cut off old columbine stems one at a time to avoid harming all those tender new leaves is enough to remind you to do the job next fall.

Q: What can I do about whiteflies on my outdoor plants?

A: Fortunately, at this time of year, you don't have to do anything. Whiteflies do not survive Montana winters outdoors. If you have them next year, you probably got them either from a greenhouse where you bought a plant or a greenhouse where your neighbors bought a plant and the insects wafted over on a breeze.

If you have indoor plants, be very careful about whiteflies. If you bring a plant in from outdoors, quarantine it for two weeks, just as you would with any new houseplant you buy. If your outdoor plants have whiteflies, wash your hands and scrub under your fingernails thoroughly when you come in to insure that you aren't transferring any whiteflies or eggs to your houseplants.

It is much easier to prevent whiteflies than to cure them.

Q: You said whiteflies don't live through the winter here. I don't believe you. How come I see them on my plants every year in August? This year they even moved indoors when I brought my houseplants in.

A: They don't live through the winter outdoors, but they do live indoors. There is no whitefly that tolerates freezing weather, period. But you now have a good example of how they survive the winter. They move inside.

You will need to get rid of your indoor infestation, or come spring they will be ready to go back out and start on your plants at the beginning of the summer, as well as at the end.

The common name of the most common whitefly is "greenhouse whitefly." That is where they like to take their room and board. You don't have to bring home any flying adult. All it takes is an egg or larva attached to the back of a leaf. Between June and August you can develop a very large population. The whitefly is one of the insects that doesn't even need a partner to reproduce.

You probably wouldn't even see the one you brought home, because both the eggs and the early stages of the larvae are too small to see with the naked eye. Only after they are about a week old, getting bigger and fatter, can you identify them if you know what you are looking for.

But you have them now and must get rid of them. The easy answer is to get rid of any houseplant on which whiteflies are feeding. A lot of your houseplants are perfectly safe because whiteflies are very picky eaters. They are extremely fond of fuchsia, but won't touch a geranium.

Pick up each plant, preferably in the late evening or early morning when they won't be flying around much. Look on the under sides of the leaves. The adults are easy to see. They are the only REALLY white insect you ever will find on a houseplant. And there won't be just one – there will be plenty.

If there are less than 10, set the plant down and look for a plant nearby that has more. Whiteflies occasionally will sit down on a plant they are not eating. As you come to a plant that is an obvious food source, pick it up carefully and carry it very gently to the nearest exit so you don't disturb them into flying to other areas of the house. Once you get rid of the plants sustaining them, within a week you should see no more whiteflies.

But suppose you don't want to get rid of the plants – one of them is a favorite of yours. You can probably get rid of the whiteflies, but you will have to work at it harder and you must keep up the good fight every single day for at least two weeks, using a variety of techniques.

If this sounds as if we are speaking from experience, that is because we are. In late August Molly brought in some cuttings of ornamental sweet potato vines. Whiteflies didn't occur to her even though sweet potato is one of their favorite entrees. A couple of weeks later, she picked up a cutting to look at and saw a whitefly. Mistake No. 2 was that after killing that one insect, she went on vacation for two weeks, leaving the sweet potato in the house.

When she returned, that bug had many, many descendants and they were having a major family reunion in her garden window. Their favorite restaurants there, besides sweet potato cuttings, were the lemon verbena, tomato and cucumber plants.

In order to harvest some more ripe tomatoes and mature cucumbers, Molly kept the whiteflies under control for about a month with weekly spraying of neem. Neem and horticultural oils get the best results on whiteflies. Insecticidal soap is only somewhat effective. And the insects have developed a resistance to any other insecticide you can buy.

She also did daily checks and got pretty good at killing them with a pinch without damaging a leaf. Also every day, she checked the leaves, especially of the tomato and cucumber, and when she found one that was a potential hatchery she clipped it off and put it out the window. She also put yellow sticky traps in the garden window. She bought hers, but you can make your own by using pieces of cardboard or wood, painted bright yellow to attract the whiteflies' attention and coated with either Vaseline or mineral oil mixed with a little dish detergent to grab their little feet. The traps need to be placed not more than three feet apart and at the same level as the whiteflies because they fly only horizontally.

We read that you can repel whiteflies from a particular plant by using aluminum foil as a pot cover, but we haven't tried that yet.

After the tomatoes were ripe and the cucumber had passed its prime, Molly got up early, cut the plants off at the ground and put them out in the cold. She sprayed the sweet potatoes and lemon verbena once more and kept yellow sticky cards near those plants for another month.

That's one of the problems in dealing with whiteflies. The eggs take a week to hatch and the larvae three to five weeks until they pupate. The books say that if adult whiteflies have no food source, they will all die within a few days. One of the things Molly learned that the books don't say is that, like a lot of insects, whiteflies are strongly attracted to light. On the days she disposed of the tomato and cucumber plants, she killed about 300 on the window next to them. The next day she annihilated thirty and the day after only one. It was a sunny day and they just sat there and let her squash them. She had sprayed with neem the day before so they may have been too sick to get up and leave.

Q: Is there anything useful to do with all these leaves?

A: Almost everyone has enormous bags of leaves and doesn't know what they can possibly do with them. Everyone they know who uses leaves has said, "No, thanks, I already have plenty." And if you put them out in the trash the landfill doesn't like you.

What you should do is put them all back on your own land. Anyone who has gardened for more than a few years knows about the value of recycling and composting to create fertile soil. Leaves have, ounce for ounce, more minerals than any other piece of a plant you could put back. They are very good for soil building. One of the things old gardeners often speak of reverently is "leafmold," which is nothing more than composted leaves – one of the richest meals you could feed your dirt.

You should feel guilty for trying to get rid of your leaves. We have news, though. We have lots of ideas for taking care of your leaves without having to work hard.

First of all, don't rake until you have to. Let the fall wind blow them around. A lot of them will blow into spaces like under trees and bushes, which are ideal places to leave them, unless they get more than a foot deep. Let them start composting in place.

If you already have raked, or can't stand looking at leaves on your lawn while waiting for the wind to blow, and you already have them in leaf bags, leave them there. Store the bags where they won't be an eyesore and let the leaves compost themselves into leafmold. Keep the bag closed. If you add a little nitrogen of some kind it will speed up the composting. Check every once in a while, especially when the weather is warm, to make sure they stay moist, because that also will speed up the process. It will take two or three years, but you don't have to do another thing; by the end of that time you will have a much smaller quantity in your bags and it will have become leafmold.

You can pile leaves several inches deep over the root area of all your trees and shrubs. In order to prevent them from matting down into a rain-shedding "roof," mix them with something like straw or shred them. You can also shred leaves before bagging them to compost and you can use shredded leaves as mulch on any flower or vegetable bed. If you don't have a power shredder, you can chop the leaves by dumping them on the lawn and running the lawnmower over them, or dump them in a garbage can and use a weed eater in the can.

If your shredded leaves are not moist, sprinkle them when you pile them somewhere, just so they will start to pack down before the next wind blows them over to the neighbor's. You could also consider piling them, preferably shredded, to make a compost pile on any area where your soil is not so great.

If none of those ideas appeals to you, there is a new way of dealing with leaves that we haven't tried but sounds good. It is called "leaf chunk mulch." It sounds like fun to make. Put leaves in a container big enough to stand in and tromp them down as much as you can. Pack them down hard. Leave them there over the winter. By spring, they are supposed to have begun the process of decay enough that you can fork out chunks about an inch thick. Just set the chunks around any place you want mulch for next summer.

While we are on the subject of mulch, we have run into the subject of newspaper mulch often enough that, although we haven't done it, we think we should mention it. This is how you turn old newspapers into weed mat that prevents weed seeds from coming up, prevents them from germinating and biodegrades into a soil amendment. You just lay the papers out about five pages thick, sprinkle them with enough water to get them to settle down onto the soil and then cover them with a layer of any kind of mulch. The paper will let moisture go through so the soil doesn't dry out. It will last about a year.

Winter

WINTER

Q: Can I grow primroses here? If I buy one at the grocery store, can I plant it in the garden later?

A: Yes and yes. There are some kinds of primroses, like the tall, Japanese candlestick kinds, that are not happy here because they need to grow on the edge of a pond. Many of those you get in the grocery store will be hardy but some will not – there is no way to tell but to try them. If you buy your plants from a nursery, they probably are hardy and the nursery person can tell you.

Most of the plants that you think of as primroses are hybrids and are plenty tough to handle our winters.

With a grocery store plant, the buds on the plant when you bought it will open; then it is done blooming. Put it in a window with good light but no direct sun. You won't buy a nursery plant until April, and that is the right time to harden off any primroses. All you will need to do is get them used to the outdoors instead of the greenhouse. This hardening-off process starts by putting the plants out for a few hours in the middle of the day for a couple of days. Gradually lengthen their stay and after a week, it should be safe to leave them out overnight.

The plant does what no person can do – toughen itself up. No matter how many weeks you tried, you wouldn't be able to stay outdoors for a week with no clothes on. But over the course of just a few days, the plant actually changes its structure, thickening its cell walls enough to handle the weather outside.

You might like to try growing primroses from seed. It's not hard, but there are rules. First, plant early – like February. Primrose seeds need some cold stratification to trick them into thinking they have been through a winter. Sow some on the surface of the soil in six packs. Dampen them from the bottom by setting them in a pan of water until the soil gets dark on top, then lift them out and let them drain. If you water from the top, the fine seed will all disappear down cracks and crevices and never be seen or heard from again.

Primrose seed needs light to germinate, so do not cover the seed at all. Just slide the six packs into plastic bags, stick them in the refrigerator and make a note on the calendar to take them out again in three or four weeks. Not being the smartest seeds in the world, they will think how nice it is to be through winter and ready for this lovely spring.

Leave them at cool house temperatures; the ideal temperature for germination is the low 60s. They need light, but not too much light. Direct sun is death to primroses.

Germination takes about a month. It's easiest to leave the pots in the same plastic bag they lived in while refrigerated. Check once a week to see if they need moisture.

If you don't see any baby green leaves in six weeks, give up, but don't necessarily blame yourself. If the seed was not completely ripe when collected, it will not germinate. It's not like carrots, whose seed will sit there in the ground, finish maturing and then germinate.

If you have some primroses now or have a neighbor with some to share, you can dig up a few seedlings this spring. Once you have an established primrose bed, the plants will keep seeding themselves. Although established plants usually develop several crowns, it is not a good idea to try to divide them. Plants grown from seed always are better than the ones coming from divisions.

Think carefully about the location you choose for primroses. A couple of years ago a man asked why he couldn't grow primroses and it turned out he was putting them on the south side of his house. They are happiest if they never get direct sunlight. If you can't find a spot like that, they will tolerate a few hours of early morning sun, but no midday or late afternoon stuff.

Q: I'm new to the area and about to start landscaping my new home here. I've heard what a problem deer can be and want to know which plants, trees and shrubs are deer-proof?

A: If you require deer-proof, we recommend plastic plants. We can't even guarantee deer haven't developed a taste for silk flowers. We don't know anything that some deer somewhere won't at least sample.

Deer behave differently in different parts of the country, so if you read in a magazine from some other section of the country that deer won't touch a particular plant, you can't depend on Montana deer to follow suit.

We just read in a very reputable book that one of the things deer don't like is tulips. Here we know that if tulips put up buds the deer will devour them so fast you'll never see what color the flowers might have become.

There are things deer like less than other things. Among trees, they prefer not to eat sharp-needled conifers, like spruce. They don't like old, prickly junipers, either, but young ones are soft enough to attract them. Many trees they don't eat unless they are very hungry. We don't know of any deciduous tree deer won't eat. They really like fruit trees and mountain ash.

From personal experience, the only shrubs deer haven't eaten are two or three kinds of currants and a flowering almond with single blossoms. They browsed a whole row of bushes and only that one almond wasn't touched. They aren't supposed to like lilacs, but they loved Molly's lilacs.

If you have a whole lot of shrubs, the deer might not browse them into the ground. It would depend on the ratio of the deer population to the plant population.

Among the flowers, deer do not like any of the narcissus family, plants with milky latex sap (poppies), ferns, foxglove, iris, lupine, the rudbeckias (coneflowers, brown-eyed susans and gloriosa daisies), Oregon grape and a lot of herbs and other plants with pungent smells like calendula, marigolds and zinnias.

Narcissus offer many species, including all the daffodils, so if you plant a wide variety you can have a bulb bed that will give you six to eight weeks of colorful bloom.

Things the deer particularly crave include roses, peonies, pansies, peas and lettuce.

Don't count absolutely on anything on this list. Everything depends on how hungry the deer are. They will also pull up a plant to see whether they might like it or not. One year, deer pulled up an entire row of cauliflower plants in our gardens and spat them out. They didn't eat them, but in the morning, the cauliflower plants were just as dead as if they had. Your best bet is protection, and the most important thing is to get there first. Deer are the most habitual of any habit-forming creatures and walk in exactly the same places for very long periods.

If you haven't seen deer or their trails, they may never discover you. But if you have put the garden on a deer path, they will go right through it. If their paths went by either side of your garden site, it could be years before they venture off the path to see what you have to offer.

Some people swear a single strand of electric fence does a fine job. (You might need two strands when fawns are around.) But if you go for electric fence, you have to remember to turn it on every single night and you must keep it in good repair. If a deer crashes into it and breaks it, you'd better get out there and fix it. We know of a man who had protected his strawberry bed for several years with an electric fence and the first time he forgot to turn it on, the deer went in and ate the first three rows. They seem never to give up checking and always remember when strawberry season is.

You can cage young trees, putting the fence far enough out so the animals can't reach the trees. Take the cages off when the trees are big enough to survive if deer eat the lower limbs. Just don't plant the trees out in the middle of your lawn unless you're prepared to mow around them with shears until the cages come off.

People have had fairly good luck putting chicken wire over low-growing things, although that doesn't look lovely. You can also crisscross fishline a foot apart over things. If you have heard you could put fishline on poles around the garden, don't believe it. The deer just keep pushing and bumping until the poles break or bend, then they step over the line and browse to their hearts' content.

As for repellents, there are a couple of sprays that won't wash off. They last six months. You must remember to wash your hands many, many times after using them and keep your fingers away from your mouth, or you will discover exactly why they are effective. They are excruciatingly bitter. Obviously, they cannot be used on food crops.

Egg spray and hair bags may do the trick for you, but after two or three years, the animals manage to adjust their tastes or priorities to a point where they can ignore those deterrents.

As long as you are just beginning your landscaping, you might seriously consider saving part of your budget for a deer fence. Generally a six-foot fence is enough to keep deer out. You can also put up two three-foot fences not more than five feet apart. The animals can jump one, but don't have enough room for take-off to jump the second. This requires twice as many fence posts and post holes, but you don't have to look at a six-foot fence. You also might fence just part of your yard where you plant the things deer like.

Q: I'm not sure I'm fertilizing my houseplants correctly. Does a cactus need a special fertilizer? What kind is best for blooming houseplants?

A: Cactuses are pretty tolerant – have to be to survive in the desert. They respond to any old thing you give them. They do better than other plants on a lean diet, but are happiest when receiving adequate water and food.

Give them the same amount you would any other houseplant.

Remember that cactuses need a resting time in winter and less fertilizer then. A lot of books say you shouldn't fertilize any houseplant in winter. We tried that once. It was not long before the plants let us know that they didn't think much of those books.

We read an article saying parsley would die if its fertilizer rate got too high, so we knocked off feeding our indoor parsley for a while. It got to looking pale and peaked, so we began fertilizing again. In about ten days the parsley perked up and has been healthy and dark green ever since.

We recommend developing a schedule for fertilizing houseplants. We do it on the first Sunday of the month and feed half strength in winter. Use whatever regimen suits you, but remember that the more often you feed, the more diluted the solution needs to be.

As for blooming plants, including cactuses, they need a lot more phosphorus than nitrogen. Nitrogen is for leaves. You may have noticed that in fertilizers made for houseplants the three nutrient numbers are about the same. Blooming plants will be much happier if the second number is quite a lot bigger than the first.

You can use ordinary garden fertilizer – our houseplants thrive on it. Use anywhere from a pinch to a couple of tablespoons, depending on pot size. Don't worry if it takes a couple of months of watering for the fertilizer pellets to dissolve.

If you opt for houseplant fertilizer administered in water, we find it best to use it every time you water, but at half strength.

Q: I bought an amaryllis bulb three weeks ago and planted it. Right away it got a little bitty green thing on top, but it's not growing. It is in the living room in a west window. Would it help to move it?

A: The west light and living room temperature should be suitable for amaryllis.

Q: I bought a bag of potting soil to plant it in. Is that OK?

A: Yes. It will be much happier in potting soil than the fiber it came packed in.

Q: I lift the pot every day and water it whenever it gets light in weight. Is that all right?

A: There is no better system. You get three stars and go to the head of the class.

Q: *The potting soil has some furry stuff on top. Will it hurt the amaryllis?*

A: It is just some unknown fungus, but it won't do the plant any damage.

Q: *Will it eventually bloom?*

A: There is no gold-plated guarantee, but we surely think it will. A lot of amaryllis seem to develop their own schedules. One we had last year sat for two months before taking off. The little green thing is probably a leaf and not a bloom stalk. It may sit there and not grow at all until the plant blooms.

 If something is wrong with the amaryllis and it doesn't bloom, you can assume it is something the grower did before you got the bulb. If you're worried about whether the bulb is healthy, poke it with your finger. If it is good and firm, it's fine.

Q: *I want to put up a fence for privacy in the back yard and am thinking some weathered boards would look nice with the house and landscaping. What type can you recommend?*

A: First, for privacy, make the fence five feet high. You still will be able to see over it and the neighbors will too, but they can't watch what you are doing unless they climb up on a step stool and peer over the top. A higher fence will not only make it look like a stockade from the outside but it will make you feel like you are living in one.

 Second, don't make a solid fence. You can put an inch to an inch and a half between boards and still have privacy. Nobody can see through unless they put their eye to the slot. You will like the effect of the light and air coming through, too. But most important is the way the fence will function as a windbreak. If some of the wind can come through the fence, it will be a very effective shelter for the plants near it because it will slow down the wind. If the wind encounters a solid wall of fence, it will blow up and over or around and in and actually will pick up speed in the process. You end up with a yard windier inside the fence than outside.

 There are a couple of other ways you can create a board fence besides nailing boards flat to the rails with spaces between the boards. One is to put all the boards at about a thirty-degree angle. This makes a fence like a partially open vertical blind. It's more complicated to do, but it allows more air to come through. You have to have a flat top and bottom board and the angled boards between them.

A third way is to alternate vertical boards with the first one on the inside of the stringers and the next one outside. You get plenty of air circulation and complete privacy.

Q: I bought an ivy and then I think I watered it too much. It didn't look good, so I repotted it. I think it's dying. Is there anything I can do to save it?

A: It sounds like you did a good job of diagnosing the problem. Ivy does not like to be too wet and repays you for your efforts by dying. But only after the mandatory two weeks of developing symptoms to confuse you and make you wonder what you did wrong yesterday.

Repotting wouldn't help. The problem with over-watering is that the roots are deprived of the air they need; the air spaces in the soil are occupied by water. In addition, wet soils provide an ideal environment for common fungi, some of which cause root rot. Unhealthy roots plus healthy fungi equal dead plants.

Occasionally – only occasionally – if you have a very tough plant, repotting can help if you shake off all soil without roots in it and put the plant into a much smaller pot. If it has been attacked by root rot, very few live roots remain and you end up with a pot that looks grotesquely small for the size of the plant.

This technique helps only if the plant has a lot of healthy looking leaves and it is never a sure thing.

Still, there is hope for your ivy, not the whole plant, but part of it, at least. Ivy is very easy to root, so the smartest thing to do is to take cuttings. Take any stem that looks healthy, cutting off between four and six inches. De-leaf the bottom half, put in a glass of water and put in a spot with good light, but no direct sun. It should root for you.

It is very easy to over-water this time of year. The days are shorter, the sun lower, light levels less, so plants are growing slower and don't need as much water as you have been giving them. If your watering system is on autopilot, it's time to switch back to manual.

Somehow, plants know when the days are getting shorter. They don't grow at the same rate when days are getting shorter as they do when the days are exactly the same length but getting longer.

You'd notice this with your ivy cuttings. They probably will take quite a long time to root now. In May, they could probably get the job done in about three days.

Q: I have a new house with zero landscaping. I know trees will be an important part of the overall plan, but how do I start?

A: Start by asking yourself a list of questions.

First, do you want conifers, which will be green in the winter, or deciduous trees that will drop their leaves and admit the maximum amount of sunlight when days are short?

Many conifers do very well here and you wouldn't be looking at something brown all winter. However, when the nights are long and the days short, everything about conifers will look dark.

Conversely, deciduous trees have no leaves to shade you when you want every available ray of sunshine, but you do have to rake their leaves. (Conifers are far from debris-free. They drop cones and needles.)

When planting a tree for shade, you need to choose the variety this year and plant it next year. Watch the sun for at least half a year and figure out where the shade will fall. Shade trees need to be placed on the south or southwest side to provide the most protection in our maximum sun times.

Do you want fast growth? Are you only interested in the shape that ultimately emerges? How tall do you want it to be?

A tree is a long-term decision. You don't want to find out in eight years that it is going to be much too big. Check the labels carefully for height and width before you buy or order it.

To give yourself an idea of how tall your tree might be, measure out on the ground the number of feet the label says it will grow. Even if it will look small and isolated at first, plant your tree for its size at maturity.

When do you want a tree to look its best? There are lots of flowering trees which give you two weeks of blossoms in the spring and fifty weeks of something else. The tree may not have a nice shape or pretty bark or lovely leaves. You might want one or two flowering trees, but not fill your yard with them.

Every tree has something it is best at. Some have attractive ball, vase, cone or asymmetrical form. Some have gorgeous leaves and are best in a place you can see them up close. Some have beautiful bark, but it usually takes several years to develop this nice quality. Bark can add color in winter when you want anything in your yard except drab brown. Plant these trees where you can enjoy them from your windows.

Some trees have lovely autumn foliage. Some have nice fruits – either to eat or to look at. Do you want a tree wildlife can use? Conifers are very good for bird nesting – birds can fly into them and virtually disappear.

Once you have answered all these queries about what you want, ask yourself just what it is you can offer the tree. You need to place it where it can be happy and not just get sicker and sicker for four or five years and then die. Trees are fairly choosy about whether they get full sun, partial sun or shade.

How is your soil? Are you planning to plant your tree in sandy loam or in a glacial moraine? Think a little bit about soil pH. If a tree requires an acid soil, you are probably not going to be able to provide it.
How much water are you able to provide and how much does it need? How much space, water and nutrients will it take up below ground? They used to say the root system of a tree was about the same size as its branch system, but it is really much bigger, especially near the soil surface. Don't plant a tree that requires a lot of water and grows a dense canopy in a place you want nice grass because in eight to ten years there won't be any grass there.

Consider exposure to wind. Trees with limber branches do OK in wind, but some are brittle and lose a lot of limbs in a stiff breeze. Where does the prevailing wind come from? You don't want to wake up in the middle of some windy night wondering if the tree is going to fall into the bedroom.

Don't forget to check to what zone a tree will be hardy. If you can offer a reasonably sheltered spot and it's supposed to be hardy to Zone 5, it will probably be all right. But if you are going to put it out on a rocky point and ask it to serve as a windbreak, it needs to be Zone 4 hardy.

Keep this list in your mind when going nursery or catalog shopping for trees. One thing about buying your trees locally is that you can ask nursery personnel how a tree will do here and what diseases or other difficulties you might expect.

Q: I have a fifteen-year-old jade plant with a trunk two to three inches in diameter. I have kept it pruned so it isn't huge, but it has an attractive shape. I water it once a week and fertilize it once a month. Last spring, some leaves began to look sick. It looked worse and worse and by July was definitely in bad shape. Thinking it might be pot-bound, my wife and I wrestled it out of the pot, but were amazed to find it had hardly any roots at all. I hosed the soil off and re-potted it in a mixture of good topsoil and driveway gravel with a layer of rocks in the bottom to aid drainage, though the pot does have a hole. About six weeks ago, it started to grow. The new leaves are small, but there are a lot of them. Do you think it's going to live? Could its problem have been too much water or fertilizer? Is there anything else I should do differently?

A: There are a lot of questions here, but several readers have asked about jade plants, so we'll try to cover several bases with this inquiry.

First, we are optimistic. It sounds like you have rejuvenated your plant very well, as indicated by its production of many new leaves.

Given the story as it developed, it is likely that water played a part in the problem. You can't really water on a rigid time schedule.

Sometimes the plant is in more active growth than others. Even if you never move it from one location to another, the light is going to change seasonally, so at one time it may get a long spell of direct sun and at others get almost all its light indirectly, which has an effect on its drinking habits. So does the temperature and humidity of your house. There are probably ten other things we haven't even heard of that make a difference, as well.

So water when the plant gets dry. In winter, when it is likely to be resting, water only when REALLY dry. With a plant that large and old you can't lift the pot to determine dryness unless you spend the rest of your time lifting weights. Stick a finger or a spoon into the soil to make sure it is bone dry an inch down. Once a week is a good schedule for checking.

A jade plant is a succulent and does well when dry. It won't up and die on you unless you forget it for a couple of months. Almost surely, as it got wetter, your plant lost vigor and root rot fungus was able to attack it. More and more roots died until few remained. This is a good example of not letting a plant be wetter than it wants to be. If you under-water, the worst that could happen is the plant would grow more slowly, but if you over-water, the worst result is death.

You were wise to realize you needed to do something for your plant, and getting it out of its pot was a good idea. Hosing off the old soil probably had no effect, positive or negative. Your use of topsoil and gravel was a good one. It is best to estimate a plant's natural soil and do your best to imitate that.

If you don't want to or can't use natural stuff, a good mixture for succulents is two-thirds potting soil and one-third sand. This lets it dry out fast enough to keep its roots from getting soggy.

The layer of rocks is something we all used to do but is no longer recommended. Just make sure your pot has a hole in the bottom and don't add anything for drainage.

Rocks take up valuable space needed for roots and nutrients. They can also create a "perched water table." This happens when you go from small soil particles to large ones like rocks. The layer just above the large ones tends to stay wet, so any time roots grow down into that layer they stay wet and get unhealthy.

We can't guarantee that fifty years form now experts won't be saying something different, but for now, we recommend filling up a pot with soil. Don't worry – the hole won't plug up.

When you water a succulent, give it a good drink, but don't let the water run out the holes into the saucer. If it does, sop that up and remember the plant will be happier if it's not too wet.

As for fertilizer, once a month is a pretty good schedule, but give your plant a lighter dose when it is growing slower.

Q: I planted my avocado in soil and now it's two feet tall. What should I do now? Must I prune it? Do I really cut off all but one leaf? Should I fertilize it? With what? How do I know when it's time to repot it? I have an ivy growing in water – do I pot that the same way as I did the avocado?

A: Unless you want its single stem to grow through the ceiling, yes, you have to prune the avocado. But think of it as being like cutting hair, not amputating an arm. Remember apical dominance? (It makes one glassy-eyed just to look at a term like that.) It means that every place along a stem where a leaf takes off has a bud sitting there. The bud is probably so tiny you can't even see it. As long as the bud at the tip is growing, the other buds along the stem remain dormant. But if you lop off the terminal bud, it lets the next one or two (occasionally even three) buds begin to grow. That's how you get branches. If only one bud grows, clip the stem off again and pray for twins.

You don't necessarily have to cut off all but one leaf. You can cut off as little or as much as you want, as long as you leave a bud or two. If you cut off all the dormant buds, there's nothing left to grow.

When deciding where to cut your plant off, sit back and look at it from all angles. Remembering that the new buds that grow will be at the bottom of branches, ask yourself where you want it to branch. There will be more new branches above, but none below. Try to imagine how it might look in a year and clip accordingly.

Yes, fertilize your avocado a bit now and then. Give it a meal or a snack of whatever you have. It cares more about being fed than what's on the menu. It is not an acid-loving plant, so don't give it a fertilizer designed to raise soil acidity. All balanced fertilizers contain nitrogen, potassium and phosphorus; those are the things needed most after light, air and water. If you want to be extra nice, give it a formula that contains some micro-nutrients, as well.

As you get to know this avocado, you'll learn its appetite. Avocados are very forgiving plants, as long as you feed them a little something. A little more often is better than a lot once in a while, but some is better than none, and too much is worse than none. It is easy to over-fertilize with commercial fertilizers because they are very concentrated. They can get a plant growing so fast that it ends up with weak, floppy stems and burned leaves.

Repot when any of these symptoms appear: it gets top-heavy and falls over; the roots become so crowded that the pot is dry at the end of each day; it starts putting out smaller leaves; or it looks silly.

The ivy question is easy. Unless you want it to live all its life in water, which it will do perfectly well, pot it up just as you did the avocado.

Q: I have read that fungus gnats are a big problem. I have them in my houseplants this winter and hadn't been really worried. Should I be?

A: The people who write about fungus gnat problems are the professional growers who are far more likely than you to have fungus gnat problems. For most of us they (the gnats, not the growers) are just those little gray specks that fly past your eyes. You bat them away with your hands and say, "Drat! Out of here!" They live in the potting soil and eat some of the decayed vegetable matter in the soil. To do damage, they would have to finish up all the food in the potting soil and start on the plant's roots. That would require a very high population. That happens in places like greenhouses and nurseries.

The larvae down in the pot do the eating. They grow up, climb out on top of the soil and fly away. It is the adults that are a nuisance to you, but they eat only very little and mostly liquids at that – water and flower nectar.

Of course in a good location, like a pot whose soil is just the way the articles recommend, consistently moist but not soggy, you have a great breeding ground. You get one generation very quickly following another year round. The easiest way to get rid of fungus gnats is to find out which pots most of them are living in and cover the surface of the soil with at least 1/4 inch of sand or fine gravel. For reasons nobody understands, this prevents the insects from crawling out. It is not an instant cure, but it is a guaranteed one.

Q: I have a spider plant and a peace lily and both have brown leaf tips. What causes that and what can I do?

A: That is both an easy and a hard question. Brown leaf tips almost always come from some sort of stress and not from any disease. The hard part is identifying the stress so you can decide on a remedy.

Those two plants are ones that get brown leaf tips easily, as do prayer plants and palms. Almost always it is the plant whose leaves end in points that get brown tips and usually it's ones with long narrow leaves. You are dealing with environmental stresses. The plants have a hard time with dry air, and by the time the Christmas season is over, everything in the house has dried out and you begin to see the effects on your plants. You don't notice it when you first fire up the furnace. The plant just can't get water to all the parts of the foliage fast enough, and the leaves evaporate the water into the dry air at a rate the roots can't replenish. Of course the tips are the last stop on the line. If it is a pointed leaf, there is not much around to help share the shock.

If dry air is the only stress it is hard to do very much. You can get a humidifier. You can group your plants together to share the moisture that they are evaporating. But that may not be the whole story. The problem may also have to do with the other end of the plant – the fine root hairs that are taking the moisture out of the potting soil and sending it upstairs. If the root hairs are not healthy, there will not be as much moisture shipped off to the leaves.

There are two things that commonly kill off root hairs. One is letting the plant get too dry in between waterings. Any time the plant dries out it will be healthy enough to survive without even showing any wilt, but the first things to go are the tiny root hairs. Another common problem is mineral salts in the potting soil. If you haven't repotted plants for a long time, the salts just keep building up. They come partly from the fertilizer you use, but also from the water. If those same plants were living outdoors you wouldn't have to worry because the salts would be continually leaching down through the soil and joining the nearest creek. But soil in a pot is a closed world and the salts have no escape.

When you get too much mineral salt in the soil, the same things happen that you learned about back in junior high science classes. The plant has inside it not pure water but a solution of sugars and salts. When you have pure water in the soil outside the plant, it flows easily through, by osmosis into the plant. But as the pure water in the potting soil gets saltier and saltier, the concentrations inside and outside the plant become more nearly the same and the water flows much more slowly into the plant, even if it is sitting in soggy soil. It's possible to get so much salt in the potting soil that the flow goes the other way and you actually dehydrate the poor plant. That means a fairly quick death.

A couple of solutions are available to you. Repot the plant, knock as much soil as possible off the roots and add fresh soil. Or try to leach out some of the salts by setting the plant in the sink and pouring fresh water through it several times, draining it to said creek via your plumbing system.

There are other things that can cause brown leaf tips, but they are not common. If you never fertilize and never repot, the plants may be just announcing that they would like some food. If you are on city water you may have noticed that lately it smells of chlorine. Many plants are sensitive to chlorine in their water. If you suspect that is the problem, the solution is easy. Every time you water, refill your watering pitcher and allow it to sit for at least 24 hours; the chlorine will be gone. It breaks down pretty fast. There also is the turn-your-back solution – you just say, "Oh, it's wintertime. My plants have brown leaf tips. It will go away next summer. If it gets too bad, I will cut off the worst spots."

Q: I got an azalea and it was the most beautiful blooming plant, but it has finished blooming. What should I do with it now? Shall I cut it back?

A: If it has been happy all the time it was blooming, just don't move it. Azaleas are notorious for being fussy about the amount of light and the temperature where they live. You might need to move it for the summertime because a window giving it the right amount of light now will be too bright for it when the sun angle changes.

As for cutting it back, the basic answer is "don't." Cut off all the dead blossoms and the brown tips where they grew. No other pruning is necessary except to maintain a pleasing shape. If it starts getting one branch that's longer than the others, you can cut it back, but cut it near the center of the plant rather than just shearing it off at the length of the other branches.

It is a good idea to look at the root system now. It may need a slightly bigger pot and this would be the time to repot it. It should start into a period of growing leaves instead of flowers and might like to make the move first. Be sure there is plenty of peat moss in the potting soil you add. Azaleas are acid lovers, and peat moss helps raise soil acidity. Since the water around here does not come from acid soil, you will have to counteract that by using a fertilizer designed for acid-loving plants – check the package labels. If you prefer to use only organic materials, you can use whatever fertilizer you otherwise use and supplement it with some horticultural sulfur sprinkled on the soil every couple of months.

As for temperature preferences, azaleas like it cool. They are most content with days about 70 and nights below 55, which may not be your idea of ideal house temperatures. Come summertime, you can either keep it in the house or put it outdoors in the shade, remembering to bring it back in again before it gets frosted. It should, all things being equal, bloom again next spring.

If your azalea gets spider mites, it is probably too hot or too dry or both. And finally, if it starts looking sick and dies on you, don't blame yourself. Florists' azaleas are not bred as long-term houseplants. They are bred to enjoy one glorious bloom and then take a quick trip to the compost pile.

Q: I have been trying for several years to grow a rosemary plant. I started by growing one outdoors in summer and bringing it inside in the fall, but the leaves curled up. Last year, I bought a plant and just kept it indoors, but the leaves still curled up. Last year, I bought a plant and just kept it indoors, but the leaves still curled up. It always has some dried leaves and some of the stems have brown areas. Is it too wet? Too dry? I always water it every Sunday until water runs through.

A: The dry leaves are dead. A live rosemary leaf looks pretty much like a dead one, so it is the dryness or stiffness that tells you it is deceased. The brown stems may be dead, and if they are at the tips of the branches that is almost surely the case. Rosemary stems naturally turn from green to brown as they age, so brown stems on a lot of the plant may simply mean they are normal stems getting woody.

The curly leaves are telling you that they are not happy. It may not be a death threat, but just their cry for help. You can aid them by knowing that the plant comes originally from the Mediterranean, so it likes its weather hot, sunny and dry. This is a hard atmosphere to achieve in the middle of a house in the middle of Montana in the middle of winter. This is why rosemary is not the easiest thing to grow here.

Put your plant near a window, preferably west or south. Mix some sand with the potting soil to increase drainage. It will happily grow in the same sort of soil a cactus likes.

You really do need to water the plant on its own schedule and not yours. It doesn't know which day is Sunday, nor does it care. The easiest thing to do is put it in a place you pass by often so you can pick up the pot every day. The day the pot feels quite a bit lighter is the day it wants a drink. The trouble with watering once a week is that if you had a cloudy week, the plant probably is not thirsty yet, in which case the extra water will set it up for root rot. But if the sun shone three or four days that week, it may have got thirsty on Thursday or Friday and you have set it up to die of drought. We all learn this the hard way and kill lots of plants on our way to knowledge.

One of the things that happens if you let a plant get REALLY dry and then water it is that none of the water actually gets to the roots. It just forms a miniature waterfall down the inside of the pot, outside the dirt ball. When it runs out the bottom, you think it's had plenty, and it really hasn't had a sip yet. You can tell if that's the case by picking up the pot after the water ran through to see if it is appreciably heavier. If it hasn't soaked up the water, put it in a pan or a sink of lukewarm water and let it stand for half an hour or at least until the air bubbles stop rising from the soil surface.

Another thing about rosemary is that its leaves have a very small surface area, making it hard for the plant to adapt to changes in light. Therefore, if your plant has been outdoors or in a greenhouse, you have to give it at least two weeks to get to the spot in the house where you want to keep it. Otherwise it is a goner for sure. Make the change very gradually, moving it from the sunny place where it was growing to someplace that gets shade for about half the day, then to one that gets full-day shade. After several days there, take it indoors to a place that gets morning sun for a week before moving it to the sunniest spot you can find. Rosemary will be able to tolerate the move, but you have to give it enough time to change its leaf structure and it can't just do that overnight.

One other suggestion. Notice how the sunlight changes on your windowsills during the changing seasons. Sometimes the spot that was in the sun in December will be in the shade in February. The changing angle of the sun makes it light up different places.

Q: *Please explain about "row covers" for root crops. You mentioned coat hangers and PVC pipe and I have no idea of what you mean about making them into a "row cover."*

A: The plastic pipe or wire (or conduit – whatever similar thing you have at hand) is used as the support for a Quonset-shaped tunnel over a row of plants.

You cut a five-foot piece and bend it into a bow – a half-circle – and stick the ends in the ground three feet apart. Space these about three feet apart along the row and cover them with a spun-bonded fabric like Reemay to make a tunnel, which will be three feet wide at ground level and tall enough for the plants to grow under.

It also is possible to make your framework of rigid PVC pipe put together with elbows and Ts. This is more expensive than the other choices, but if yours is to be a permanent construction, it will last a long time. It is rigid and very strong.

Whatever you use, what you are creating is a physical barrier so that damaging insects can't get at your vegetables. For root crops, the biggest worry is root maggots. The covers need to be put on early in the summer to keep out the flies that lay eggs on the plants, hatch into maggots, crawl down the stems and feast on the roots. For a lot of root crops, if you get them on while the plant is still two to three inches high, you should be early enough. But for radishes, we recommend you cover them as soon as the first leaves unfold.

These covers also are good for late plantings of cabbage-family plants likely to be attacked by a late-summer hatch of root maggots, like a July planting of broccoli for a fall crop.

Also, the covers on cabbage, broccoli, Brussels sprouts and cauliflower keep the cabbage butterflies from laying the eggs that hatch into voracious green cabbage worms. For those, put the covers on as soon as you see the very first white butterfly.

The advantage of the covers is that you never have to spray for anything. Keeping the adults from laying their eggs on your plants prevents the life cycle from getting started – the caterpillars never get to your plants to damage them.

If you want to practice integrated pest management, the physical barrier is the first thing to try before going on to any kind of spray or other treatment. Let the adults fly over to your neighbor's garden or die of starvation, whichever comes first.

The goal of row covers is the creation of an insect-free haven where your plants will grow all the way to harvest. If possible, get summer-weight row cover material because it transmits the most light. If that's not available, standard weight is OK, but don't use heavy weight if the plants are to spend the entire season under it. It restricts the light and doesn't admit much water. The heavy weight is great for modifying the temperatures at the beginning and end of the growing season. Plants are OK under it for a week or two, but not for the whole summer.

Q: How do I decide which plants to put some mulch on?

A: Mulch all perennial and woody plants their first year. Mulch any plant that is marginally hardy here. If it is something you REALLY want to grow and you aren't sure it's tough enough, mulch it every year. If you mulch something that didn't need mulching, you won't really have hurt anything but your work schedule.

Other plants you might want to mulch are those in a place where they would think that the first warm days in winter meant spring – like at the base of a south or west wall. They could start to put up shoots and then get killed by the next hard freeze.

A good thick mulch (four to six inches) in places like that will be enough to keep plants from leafing out until it really is spring. When in doubt, mulch.

Q: A friend gave me some seeds of annual poppies last fall. Should I scatter them around and just rake them in or what? Should I do it as soon as the snow melts?

A: If the snow is still here on the first of June, you had better sow them in the snow banks. If it melts off before the Ides of March, that's too early. Realistically, any time from March on is a pretty good time for poppies, although they may not germinate for a while. They are tough seeds.

Do scatter and rake, but in the opposite order. Rake the soil first and then scatter the seeds, but don't rake again, because if you cover them, none will come up. Poppy seeds are one of the kinds that require light for germination.

Once they have established themselves in your garden, you don't even have to worry about gathering seed to keep the patch going. Just let them drop their seeds and they will over-winter, sprouting in the spring. The biggest problem with an established bed of annual poppies is that you have to thin vigorously every year.

Q: My hoya is taking over the living room. If I prune it , will it die?

A: No, it certainly won't. Hoyas don't mind being pruned at all and it is easy to do. They don't even sulk after you cut off the unwanted pieces. You can shape it to whatever size fits your space without thinking you have to make a choice between Jack's beanstalk and a dead plant.

You may have heard the old gardener's tale that you must leave the blossom spurs if the plant is ever going to bloom again. That is not true. If you leave them, the plant will bloom again right there, and the spur gets a little longer each time another flower cluster comes at that spot. But if you cut it off, the plant will bloom elsewhere and make more flowering spurs. Once a hoya is old enough to have flowered (which sometimes takes several years) it will flower again. Some species of hoya drop the entire flowering spur as well as the dead flower cluster and make a new spur when they get ready to bloom again.

Q: I have had a mother-in-law's tongue for ten years and have a sentimental attachment to it. It has always done fine and behaved the way it should, surviving and acting happy, no matter what you do to it. My son has taken over the watering, and suddenly it is not only unhappy, but ill to the point of death. It seems to be drying out. The leaves are limp and have fallen over like rabbits' ears.

A: We are sorry to say that your little helper may have been too generous. Many a gardener has learned to his sorrow that you can lose a plant by giving it just one more little drink.

As a succulent, too much water is the one thing that will kill a mother-in-law's tongue (a.k.a. snake plant, a.k.a. sansevieria). Succulents seem almost unkillable – they can do with very little water and are not fussy about light, although if you give them more light they grow faster.

We suspect your sansevieria has burst all its pipes and its water system is down. So, strange as it may sound, your plant probably is dying of drought. Here's what happens when the soil gets too wet, with water in the spaces that should contain air. Any number of common fungi, which float around all the time and live in the same soil with the plant, suddenly have a population explosion and overwhelm the roots. All the piping blows up like uninsulated plumbing in a Montana cold snap, and no water can get up to the leaves.

OK, but what next?

Sometimes it can be cured. In the case of this plant where all the leaves have gone limp, the fungus has progressed pretty far. The safest thing to do is make leaf cuttings and try to re-start the plant from those. Chop off sections of leaf – the book says three inches is the ideal size. You don't have to have the leaf tip, so if you have a nine-inch section of quite good leaf, you can cut it in three. Leave it sitting out on the table for an hour or so to let the cut edges dry. Then stick the bottom half-inch of each piece into a pot of rooting medium – sterile potting soil, vermiculite, sand – everybody has a favorite. You can put them close together in the same pot if you like. Keep the rooting medium damp, but not soggy. Do not fertilize at all because an overdose of fertilizer can kill off baby roots just forming. Do not cover with plastic – succulents require good air circulation. And be patient. A little prayer or a few good incantations couldn't hurt. If the cuttings are going to succeed, they will eventually start growing baby plants next to them.

The other thing you can do is to see if the poor old plant would like to grow a new top. Take it out of the pot and check the roots. If some still look healthy, you can cut off all the unhealthy ones – dark, slimy or soft – and repot the plant in a fairly small container so there is only about half an inch of unoccupied dirt around the root ball.

And either reclaim the watering can or have a serious talk with your son, explaining that bathing is good and swimming is wonderful but drowning is not so nice.

If you are successful at growing babies from the cuttings, they may not be marked like the parent. People used to think this was because you were using a piece of leaf; if you used a whole leaf the new plant would look like its mom. Research has shown this to be untrue. The process is very, very complicated, but sansevieria is capable of changing its variegations at a whim. Nobody knows what the whim is, but it may have something to do with the SIZE of the leaf cutting.

Q: My Christmas cactus bloomed every winter until I repotted it. It didn't bloom last year and not this year either, although I moved it to the kitchen where the light isn't as bright in October. I dry it out. Did I do something in the repotting that made it stop blooming?

A: No, the repotting didn't cause it, unless you put it in a pot that is much too large. Christmas cactuses have small root systems, so they don't need a very big pot. Almost certainly the problem is that your kitchen has decent light every evening when you're at home. When that cactus has longer hours of light than of darkness, it makes leaves instead of flowers. Drying it out won't hurt it, but it is not really necessary to get it to bloom. Your cactus is not nearly as fussy about evening light as a poinsettia, but you can either turn out the light as soon as you finish the dishes, or move the plant somewhere else in the house. If it gets nothing but dim light or darkness, it might bloom for you in March or April.

Q: I bought a beautiful kalanchoe in a flower shop. It finished blooming and I have not been able to get it to rebloom. Is there something I can do?

A: Kalanchoes are short day plants and are fussier about light than Christmas cactus. You might want to put a box or black plastic bag over it from dinnertime to breakfast every day. After about a month you should be able to see buds starting to form. Keep putting it to bed every night until it's in full bloom, then uncover it and it will keep on blooming.

If you have a sunny window in a place in your house where nobody will turn on a light in the evening, you don't have to go through the routine of covering the plant. Just be sure that it gets no evening light.

Q: My old gloxinia has a gigantic tuber. How can I propagate it to make sure it keeps going?

A: There are actually four ways.

1. You can propagate using the plant's seed, but this is not the way you want to do it because you want a clone, not an offspring.

You could buy seeds of a gloxinia that looks like yours. This is recommended only if you have experience growing plants from seeds the size of dust.

2. You can cut a leaf and root it as you would an African violet, to which the gloxinia is a first cousin. To grow a new plant from a leaf, you will need at least half an inch of stem, preferably more. It can be rooted in potting soil or water. One favorite way is to cover a glass of water with aluminum foil, poke a hole in the foil and put the leaf stem through it into the water. Once the roots get going, pot it up with potting soil. Eventually you will get a baby plant growing at the base of the leaf; the leaf later dies.

3. You can also take a tip cutting – a piece of stem with at least two pairs of leaves. Plant it in dirt and it will grow. In this case, the original leaves don't die.

4. The last way is to cut a wedge out of the tuber, being sure you have an eye in the piece. This won't hurt the parent plant. Dust the cut edges with sulphur or other fungicide.

However you decide to propagate your gloxinia, except rooting a leaf, drape plastic over it to keep the humidity high. In cool weather it is helpful to have bottom heat. It takes some time to get started – six or seven months.

A big gloxinia tuber can live fifty years. But if you have had a gloxinia die on you in three years or so, don't blame yourself. They are bred for the beauty of the flowers and many are not as tough as the old fashioned ones.

Q: How can I make my poinsettia into a tree?

A: Recipe: 1. One leftover poinsettia. 2. One eight- or ten-inch pot. Put one into two now. Keep it moist until the Fourth of July or whenever it starts making shoots along the stem. Let them get one inch long, then cut the tips off and leave a little stub. Stake the plant when the need arises.

You will get a taller, lanky stem with no leaves. You want eight to ten shoots at the top and the rest of the stem with little short stubs. Sometime in mid-summer, pinch out the center, leaving eight or ten side shoots.

In late summer cut off all the little stubbies. In September, prune the branches left on top, leaving two or three leaves on the top ones and three or four leaves on the lower ones. Begin treating it as you would any poinsettia you want to re-bloom, giving it at least twelve hours and ten minutes a day of absolute darkness and days of bright light.

The times and numbers of branches are not set in cement – use your own judgment. You should get a topiary poinsettia, which can be quite spectacular.

Q: Spider mites on my houseplants have been a problem for a long time. They don't seem to affect things like the succulents, but the plants they do bother just keep dying and getting thrown away. Every so often I think I have finally got them all and the first thing I know they are back. Is there an answer?

A: The good news is that spider mites are very easy to kill. The bad news is that it's not easy to keep them dead. It isn't that they are immortal, but they have a couple of things going for them.

First is their highly effective reproduction. You can kill a whole generation with one treatment, but you must keep after them for several weeks running to stop the succession.

Also in their favor is the fact that they live here and they like it. They aren't like some imported pest that once you get rid of it it's gone. They stay out in the yard all summer, but when fall rolls around, they move in to spend the winter with you. The easiest and cheapest remedy is plain water. Wash the entire plant thoroughly in the kitchen sink. If it's too big to lift, use a spray bottle. The only catch is that you must do this twice a week for several weeks.

Or you could use Cinnamite, insecticidal soap, homemade oil spray, neem or horticultural oil spray once a week. None of these will hurt you or your cat or the neighbor's kid. A few beneficial insects may be harmed by neem, but they are most unlikely to be on houseplants.

You might even consider buying predatory mites, but they are fairly expensive and you'd only want to do that if you have several good plants that are badly infested. They eat only spider mites, so once you introduce them to yours, they chow down until the spider mites are all gone and then they starve to death. They can be ordered from places specializing in biological controls.

The real secret to control of spider mites is to discover why plants are unhappy enough to succumb. They are either too hot, too dry or both. First ask yourself which is your problem, then ask yourself where you could move the plants to make them happier. If nothing occurs to you and as long as you're talking to yourself anyway, you might have to ask if it's time to compost the plants and try something different. They could just be plants so sickly that the first mites to find them tie napkins around their necks and send out luncheon invitations to all their friends.

Q: I have scale on my weeping fig, of which I am very fond. (The tree, not the scale.) So far all I have done is scratch them off now and then. What can I do to get rid of them?

A: Scratching is a good thing to do. You are keeping the numbers low and the plant should do fine, even if you don't get rid of every last one.

Scale is not common on houseplants. You probably bought or were given a fig that already had it. There are two types of scale called "soft" and "armored." The differences are mostly academically interesting. Soft scale is just as hard as armored scale.

To see which kind you have, scrape one off and look at the back. (You will probably need a hand lens and good light – no scale is very big.) If the insect stayed on the plant and just the shell came off, you have armored scale. If it is soft scale, the critter will be in the shell with its legs waving around.

If there is no creature left on the plant or in the shell, it's an old, dead scale. The shells stay on the plant for a long time after the beastie dies. You may not have as many live ones as you fear.

Some plants have bumps that look like scale, but if you scratch a bump off and find just live tissue under there, it's not scale.

Both hard and soft scale lay eggs that hatch into babies that suck juice from the plant. Those little suckers grow up to be egg-layers. Any time you scrape a scale off, you have killed it because you have destroyed its mouth parts. It can't re-infect that plant or any other.

Another reason to scrape off scale is to see if there are recently laid eggs under it. Turn over a few and look under the armor but around the outside edge. Check about once a week until you see that some have hatched – babies will be wiggling. (Hand lens required again.) Then check every day until you see some out migrating. This is the day you spray the plant with insecticidal soap or horticultural oil. It is the only time any treatment can get to the insect.

While you are doing this, cut down on your plant's nitrogen. Scale is most fond of plants with lots of nitrogen. Don't be too generous with fertilizer and use only slow-release nitrogen. Or instead of giving it a good shot of fertilizer once a month, give it a quarter of a shot every week. This will help keep the scale population from growing very fast.

Q: My corn plant (dracaena or cordyline) has grown to twelve feet and reached the ceiling. Can I cut it off without killing it?

A: Yes. Presumably it has all its leaves at the top and a very long trunk. You can cut it quite close to the ground if you want and let it start over, or you can cut it off at an attractive height and it will begin growing from the nearest bud.

To hedge your bets, you can cut the top off the stem and plant that. Just put it in a pot in moist soil and cover it with a plastic bag. Set it in bright light, but not in direct sun or you will poach it. It should root in about a month.

If you want to go into the corn plant growing business, you can cut the rest of the trunk into short sections, bury them halfway in moist soil in pots and treat them the same as the planted top. Remember, when propagating plants, a 50 percent success rate is the average.

Q: Can I do my pruning with electric hedge clippers?

A: Not now. Electric hedge clippers are used to prune formal shapes, like topiaries or shrubs that look like cones or gum drops, not to give a naturalistic form.

Trimming with an electric clipper is done during the growing season and repeated about once a month to clip off all new growth and maintain the desired shape.

Q: Help me quick! My almost-new weeping fig is dropping a lot of leaves. What have I done?

A: Most tropical houseplants need to grow new leaves when they move from any greenhouse to any home. Your Ficus is only doing what comes naturally.

The weeping fig is one of the fastest plants at doing this – it takes it only a couple of weeks. If you had got a palm tree, you probably wouldn't even notice the leaf drop happening because it takes most of a year.

Q: What can I do to help my houseplants get through these short, dark days? They are beginning to look tired.

A: When not much light is available, you need to take advantage of every lumen you can capture. First, get out the window cleaner. Clean windows let in more light than dirty ones and at this time of year your heating system may be depositing grunge on the glass.

Unscreened windows let in more light than screened ones, so if you don't take your screens off in the fall, consider doing so.

Where can you put your houseplants, besides in a little row on the windowsill? Right beside a window is often quite dark. It is usually brighter farther away from the window but directly in front of it.

Pick a day and spend some time looking at where the light hits the floor or bounces off the wall. This will give you an idea of where to put plants.

Height from the floor makes a difference. A place where a tall plant might do just fine, a short one might not. If you need to add height, set the plant on a box or stool to take advantage of available light. Placing a plant in the right spot near a mirror can provide a lot of reflected light. You also can get incandescent plant lights suitable for use as accent lamps.

You are already considering the seasonal variations. A plant getting direct sun now might be in shadow in summer when the sun is higher and the eaves shade the house.

When plants are low on light, you need to take the best possible care of all their other needs. They will tolerate less-than-ideal light if they are otherwise very healthy.

If you want a plant in a certain place because it looks good, even though the light is not the best, consider rotating two or more plants between that spot to the best natural light or to plant grow lights. Once one looks its absolute, robust best, put it back on the credenza and take its time-share partner to the light for a while.

Q: I know this is the time I should get out and prune my trees and shrubs, but I've never done it and am really nervous about chopping things off. Would it be worth the expense to hire the job done?

A: We herewith present a Pruning Primer for the Apprehensive.

Pruning is required for woody plants – those that live from year to year and do not die back to the ground in the winter. This means mostly trees and shrubs.

You can face the task, but what with? There are three basic tools.

First, you need pruning shears. They look like tough scissors and are for things up to half an inch in diameter. They come in anvil and bypass types, both operated by squeezing the handles. The anvil type has only one blade, which comes down on a flat metal surface. Bypass types have two blades, like scissors. They cost more, but they last enough longer and work enough better to be worth the extra money.

For branches up to an inch in diameter, you need lopping shears. They have small blades, like pruning shears, but their handles are about two feet long, giving you added leverage and allowing you to reach higher and into less accessible places.

The other instrument you need is a pruning saw for things larger than an inch in diameter. It cuts fast and is designed to cut on the pull stroke, rather than the push stroke like regular woodworking saws. It is usually a half-moon shape blade that folds into the handle.

It is possible to prune using kitchen shears, side-cutting pliers and a woodworking saw, but if you have several plants to do, it is much easier and more efficient to have good tools.

The basic principle of pruning is to do it sooner, rather than later. The smaller the pieces you take out, the easier it is on the plant – and on you. Don't put it off until next year.

If you prune spring-bloomers like lilacs or forsythias now, you will cut off some flower buds, but if the bush is a funny shape now, it will look better in the spring without those few flowers.

Begin by cutting out all dead branches. On deciduous trees, dead limbs are a different color from live ones – usually more gray. If you're not absolutely sure, scrape the branch with the blade of your shears and see if there's green under the bark.

Second, cut off all branches growing toward the center. You want all branches to point to the outside. Cut all but about a quarter inch at the bottom, leaving the bark collar so you won't make an open wound in the trunk itself. Leave more than that and the stub will grow a whole forest of little sprouts.

Your third task is to ferret out any branches that cross each other and could rub in the wind. Take out the skinniest one or the one with an unattractive shape, cutting all the way back to the bark collar.

By this time, your tree or bush should be looking better. Stand back, look at it critically and ask yourself if any branches are still too close together to look good or too thick to allow plenty of light to reach the leaves that will grow in the center. If the answer is yes, thin some more. A cut that takes out whole branches and lets in light and air is called a thinning cut.

Look at the plant again to see if it looks lopsided. If it does, fix it. This time you will do not a thinning cut but what is called a heading cut, taking out only the part of the branch that sticks out too far. With a heading cut, clip back to where there is a V in the branch.

On shrubs, thinning cuts should be made all the way to the ground. You can easily cut out a quarter or a third of the branches with good results. Try always to remove the biggest, oldest branches.

When it looks good, quit.

When you haven't done much pruning, it is much more likely that you will have taken off too little than too much.

There are certain things that are indicative of bad pruning.

Ends that die back come from not cutting a limb back to the bark collar on a thinning cut or to a V in a heading cut. With most trees and shrubs, if you leave a stub, there is nothing – no bud – from which it can grow. All the end of the branch can do is die.

If you leave a really short stub, you just get the aforementioned forest. You may have seen an apple tree with one or more four-inch bumps on its limbs – fist-sized bumps of bark-covered wood. These don't damage the tree, they just look ugly.

Another pruning boo-boo is the large wound. You are most likely to get this with pruning that should have been done five years earlier. When you have to cut off a four-inch branch, it will take at least two years to heal; during this time you will have an opening for disease organisms to move in and set up housekeeping.

A third indication of careless pruning is a tear. You don't get one until the branch is big enough to require a saw and the weight is enough to rip the bark back when the cut nears completion and the limb falls. With a branch large enough to require a saw, start on the bottom and cut up a quarter of the way before beginning your cut down from the top.

Remember that pruning stimulates growth and the plant is going to start growing at the first opportunity. It may look great when pruning is just finished, but unless you consider what it will be like with its new growth, you will have to shear it every year.

Any kind of pruning done fast is not going to look as nice in the long run as a job done slowly by hand.

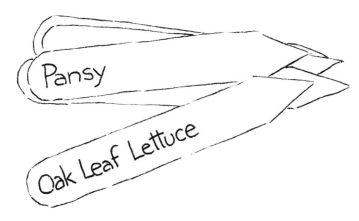

Q: My houseplants are dusty. What is the best way to clean the leaves?

A: Plant leaves do need to be kept clean because the plant "breathes" through them. The bottoms of the leaves are no problem, but the upper surfaces do get plugged up. For a plant, it's like allergy season when only half your nose works.

Smooth-leaved plants may be cleaned with a rag dampened in plain water. A little soap may be added, if you want, but it must be very diluted. Some plants mind soap more than others.

One old gardeners' wives' tale called for cleaning leaves using milk – probably because it would leave them shiny. It is probably OK, as long as you use skim milk – you don't want to leave fat on the leaves.

For fuzzy leaves, you can sweep them with a soft, clean brush, like a paintbrush. Or you could put the hose on the "blow" end of the vacuum and blow the dust away.

If your African violets get white water rings on their leaves, they can be washed. The only danger lies in letting the sun hit the wet leaves. A water drop caught in the leaf hairs acts as a prism and burns a spot on the leaf. Keep the violet out of the sun until the leaves are completely dry.

Q: The kids want to plant some popcorn and ornamental corn this year. Will it affect the flavor of our sweet corn?

A: It would if it had the chance. However, if you plant an early sweet corn and the earliest popcorn or ornamental corn available, they would mature about forty-five days apart.

Good luck getting any popcorn or ornamental corn to mature here. It might work if you have the most advantageous microclimate and conditions are exactly right.

Cross-pollination can be a real problem for sweet corn and since it is pollinated by the wind, the pollen can travel quite a distance. When planting more than one variety of corn, the best defense against cross-pollination is to choose ones that have at least a week's difference in their days to maturity.

Q: Four days ago I got a gorgeous gardenia full of blooms and buds. Two days ago I found it covered with black aphids. I sprayed the plant with a mixture of garlic and cayenne in water. Now my husband says the bugs are dead, but I don't think they are. What should I do next?

A: Probably the best thing you did was spray with water. (If they are Cajun aphids, they may actually have enjoyed the garlic and cayenne.) Water is a very good first attack against aphids, but you must go on spraying every other day for at least a week because they go on hatching.

All you are really doing is washing off the bugs. Use room temperature or barely lukewarm water. Put the pot in the sink and use the faucet sprayer if you have one. Thoroughly spray all leaf surfaces. After a week's spraying, inspect the plant very carefully every day for another week and if you see even one aphid, wash the plant again.

Nurseries tend to use systemic insecticides to keep populations under control, but the pests have caught on to their tactics and have developed immunity, or at least reduced susceptibility.

Gardenias are very touchy, especially when they are in bloom. Even if the foliage could survive treatment with an insecticide, the blossoms almost surely would not.

So keep up the water – only showers and inspections. It gets very boring looking for aphids, but you will feel so good on days you don't find any.

As to whether they are alive or dead, dead ones look white and you will see little white shells lying around under the plant.

The fact that the healthy bugs are black means only that that's the kind of aphids they are. Like the shoes in the catalog, aphids come in various colors – black, brown, green and white.

Don't worry about how your plant got the insects. If you had it only two days before they showed up, they came with the gardenia. With any luck, it won't have any more, once you get rid of them. As for other plants, make sure the gardenia doesn't touch other plants, opening a broad aphid highway for them to use for immigration. Aphids are quite specific and probably your gardenia aphids don't have a taste for your Swedish ivy anyway.

Q: Oh, dear! What's going to happen to my shrubs and trees in this warm weather? They will bud out and then they will die.

A: Only an exceptionally stupid plant is going to do this. Most trees, bushes and perennials are a lot smarter than that. Botanists know plants have a built-in timing mechanism, although they don't understand how it works. Any plant able to survive in this climate longer than three summer months is not going to be taken in by any thermometer saying, "Wake up! It's time to get growing." It pays more attention to the length of the days. It requires the right combination of day-length and temperature to set off its annual alarm clock.

So don't worry about the temperatures, but do check moisture. Your plants are not using much moisture because they are not actively growing and not as much evaporates in cold weather, but our dry winds are very desiccating. February and March are times here when plants can easily die of drought. If the soil is dry to a depth of about an inch, give the plant or tree a drink.

Q: Can I get my florist's chrysanthemum to rebloom?

A: Florist's chrysanthemums can't be treated like the ones bought to plant outdoors. Garden mums are hardy, but in most parts of North America the florist's varieties are not. They are short-day plants, like Christmas cactus and poinsettia. Their ancestors bloomed in the fall when days got short and nights long. You must create an illusion to get them to bloom.

When your plant starts looking ratty, cut all the stems back to half their length and pinch off any flower buds that remain. You want the plant to make a whole bunch of leaves. When you water and fertilize it, it will make a lot of new shoots. When they are four to five inches long, pinch off the tips – you are aiming for a short, fat, bushy plant. Pinching makes it put out new shoots again. When that crop is four or five inches long, take a critical look – if it's still not bushy enough to suit you, go through the pinching routine again. If it looks good, you can start pretending it's fall.

Give the plant thirteen to fifteen hours of night per day. This doesn't mean a dim corner like a Christmas cactus would appreciate. It means total dark, like a poinsettia demands. Unlike a poinsettia, mums need night temperatures of 60 to 70 degrees. Too warm or too cool and it will refuse to bloom. Get it out each day and put it in a nice, sunny window. Chrysanthemums don't take as long to bloom as poinsettias. You should see flower buds in eight to ten weeks.

Whether you decide to go through all this may depend on any of several factors: how attached you are to the chrysanthemum; how well you like chrysanthemums in general; how much you enjoy a challenge; how interested you are in outsmarting a plant; how important it is to prove you can do the same thing with your plant that a florist can do with his.

Q: I know my Boston fern needs repotting, but the last one I tried to divide died on the operating table. How do you recommend doing this job?

A: Repotting a Boston fern is not the easiest thing in the world to do. The stems of the fronds are very brittle, and each time you touch the plant, you break another one. Besides that, there is just no way to break apart that root ball.

We have decided you just can't worry about breaking a few fronds and all you can do with the root ball is cut it into pieces. Line up homes for the new plants ahead of time or it will soon look as if you are living in Costa Rica.

Try this: Lay newspapers on the floor or counter. Pull the plant out of the pot and roll the paper around all the fronds – everything above the soil level.

Then take a large, sharp kitchen knife and a deep breath and cut into the root ball. It will probably have several visible divisions. Cut them apart, making sure each one has some little fiddleheads in it. Then unroll the top and re-roll each division so you can repot it. Remove the paper when it's all settled in and ready to water.

If you have wondered what those long, fuzzy, wiry things are in your fern, they are rhizomes – another way the fern has of increasing itself. You can place a pot of moist soil within reach of the fern and pin the end of each rhizome down in the dirt. (Does your granny have any old-fashioned hair pins you could borrow?)

The rhizomes are similar to strawberry runners or the little plantlets on a spider plant.

Q: I think I want to buy a greenhouse. How much will I have to spend and what do I look for?

A: If you want a greenhouse and not just a cold frame tall enough to stand up in, it will probably cost a minimum of $2,000. Unless you want a fancy conservatory, it will be between there and $10,000, although it certainly is possible to spend a lot more.

Before you actually start shopping, you need to ask yourself a number of questions – and give yourself the honest answers.

First, what do you want to do with your greenhouse? Do you want to raise vegetables for your table over a longer season? Do you intend to specialize in raising orchids? Have you always wanted to grow your own grapefruit tree? Are you looking for more space for houseplants or to raise ones needing more sun than you get in the living room window? Do you want to have flowering plants to decorate your home year round? Are you planning to raise things for sale on a small scale? Do you want a place you can sit and read, surrounded by your plants?

You can't get everything from one greenhouse. If the temperature is right for cineraria in winter, you won't be able to sit in it without a coat. The biggest problems arise when people are not quite clear about what they really want and what they can do without. They try to compromise to fulfill two purposes and wind up with a structure unsatisfactory for either.

You also need to decide between a free-standing greenhouse and one attached to your house – there are only those two basic types.

Are you sure you have a good place for your greenhouse? Ideally, a site would allow a long side of the structure to face due south. You want it to be protected from the wind. The best possible situation is with deciduous trees nearby to give summer shade in the hottest part of the day and let the sunshine through in the winter. If the only place you have is on the north side of the house, save your money – or use it to move to another house with a better site.

If you can bear to wait that long, it really would pay to take a full year and keep track of just what the sun does through all the seasons.

Now, what to look for.

What size do you want and what size can you afford? As with a lot of other things, there is no such thing as too much space. However, eight by ten feet is an absolute minimum. If you are looking for anything smaller, stick with cold frames. And, however long your greenhouse is, it must not be narrower than eight feet.

In a greenhouse that is smaller, the proportion of square feet of plantable area to square feet of glazing is too small. You can't put enough plants in it to justify paying to heat all that surface.

What kind of foundation will you put under your greenhouse? It can be set on landscape timbers or on a poured foundation with a heat sink underneath. The difference is price.

One thing you don't read much about is the importance in this climate of insulating the perimeter to keep the soil inside from freezing or being influenced by the frozen soil outside.

Insulation can be something as simple as digging down a foot or two all around and putting in a barrier of foam insulation. Or you could go as deep as the ground ever freezes – about five feet – which is an enormous project. The opposite problem of overheating in the summer is not as bad here in our climate as the books tell you.

You will be choosing between an aluminum frame and a wooden one. There are advantages and disadvantages to both. Aluminum transmits heat out in winter. Wood eventually will rot from the continual moisture. There is no significant difference in price.

There are several choices of glazing material – the stuff that lets the light in. You may opt for glass or one of several different kinds of plastic. There is no one perfect surface. There are differences in price, strength and transmission of light and heat. You want something cheap that lets in 100 percent of the available sunlight, keeps in all the heat produced inside and is very strong. There is no such thing.

It is advisable to avoid using curved glass. Not only is it extremely expensive, it is often not available locally. Therefore, if you break a piece, you will be in for a long wait for a replacement, closely followed by a very large bill. Flat glass can be replaced by local firms at a more reasonable price.

Personally, we would not choose fiberglass because it has the shortest life span of light transmission before turning opaque. Look for a material that will admit at least 90 percent of available light. If your glazing admits less than 80 percent, there's no reason to have a greenhouse – your plants would do as well on your living room windowsill.

It probably does not make sense in this climate to spend money on a greenhouse unless you have a double-walled one, which means you will have two layers of stuff blocking sunlight. Specifications for any greenhouse kit will give you the percentage. None will be perfect, but some are better than others.

The other glazing consideration is heat transmission. Remember that you will be paying heating costs in winter and cooling bills in summer. Consider how much supplemental heat you can afford. Your heat can range from passive solar to completely automated electronic heaters.

Be sure the greenhouse you choose is strong enough to stand up to our wind, unless you are in an unusually well protected spot. It also must withstand an occasional hailstorm. You don't want to hear the tinkle of greenhouse glass along with the clatter of hail on your roof.

You will also pick a shape, probably either a slanted south wall or a vertical wall with a sharply slanted roof panel. Shape is very important here because our sun gets so low in the winter. It's not hard to provide some summertime shade using shadecloth, either inside or out, or an easily removable paint. Pointed arch or Quonset shapes are harder to ventilate in a home greenhouse.

Speaking of ventilation, you will need a lot of it, both to keep temperatures below 100 degrees on sunny afternoons and to control the humidity that fosters fungus problems.

Check the specifications for the amount of ventilation compared with the square feet of growing area. There are several otherwise good greenhouses on the market that do not offer adequate ventilation. The square feet of vent space should be at least one-fifth that of the floor area. Without sufficient ventilation, your plants will cook, mold or rot.

There are several good books on the subject of greenhouses and we recommend you read at least one before you make your final decision. Try not to drool on the pages.

    Greenhouses are great grown-up toys!

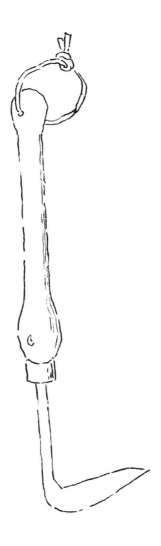

Index

LISTING OF BOOKS

Additional copies of **A YEAR IN THE GARDEN,** *and many other of Stoneydale Press' books on nature, outdoor recreation, big game hunting, history, or reminisces centered around the Northern Rocky Mountain region, are available at many book stores, gift shops and sporting goods stores, or direct from Stoneydale Press. If you'd like more information, you can contact us by calling a Toll Free number,* **1-800-735-7006,** *or by writing the address at the bottom of the page. Here's a partial listing of some of the books that are available:*

Nature/Outdoors

The Elk Mystique, *By Mike Lapinski, large format, magnificently beautiful all-color presentation in photo and text of the story of the wapiti, the American elk. Softcover, 144 pages.*

Self Defense For Nature Lovers: Handling Dangerous Situations With Wild Critters, *By Mike Lapinski, 144 pages, softcover, provides insight and tips on handling yourself in potentially dangerous situations involving mountain lions, grizzly bears, black bears, poisonous snakes, alligators, other wild critters.*

Cookbooks

Camp Cookbook, *Featuring Recipes for Fixing Both at Home and in Camp, With Field Stories by Dale A. Burk, 216 pages, comb binding, comprehensive book of preparing meals both at home and in the outdoors.*

Cooking for Your Hunter, *By Miriam Jones, 180 pages, comb binding, recipes on eating naturally. Variety of recipes.*

That Perfect Batch: The Hows & Whys of Making Sausage and Jerky, *By Clem Stechelin, 116 pages, comb binding. An authoritative, step-by-step, book on utilizing wild game in the making of sausages and jerky. Many photographs.*

Historical/Reminisces

Lewis And Clark In The Bitterroot, *By The Discovery Writers. Detailed presentation in text, photograph and illustration of the famous Expedition during its two visits to the Bitterroot Mountains in 1805-06. Color section. Hardcover and softcover editions*

Lewis And Clark On The Upper Missouri, *By The Discovery Writers. Detailed presentation in text, photograph and illustration of the famous Expedition on its travels in the Upper Missouri River region in 1805-06. Color section. Hardcover and softcover editions.*

Montana's Bitterroot Valley, *By Russ Lawrence with Photography by Harry June and others, 8½x11-inch full color book on the beautiful and historically significant Bitterroot Valley in southwestern Montana. Hardcover and softcover editions.*

Indian Trails & Grizzly Tales, *By Bud Cheff Sr., 212 pages, stories of the wilderness by a long-time, master outfitter-outdoorsman, available in clothbound and softcover editions.*

They Left Their Tracks, By Howard Copenhaver, *Recollections of Sixty Years as a Wilderness Outfitter, 192 pages, clothbound or softcover editions (One of our all-time most popular books.)*

More Tracks, By Howard Copenhaver, *78 Years of Mountains, People & Happiness, 180 pages, clothbound or softcover editions.*

Copenhaver Country, By Howard Copenhaver. *A delightful collection of stories from out of the Ovando, Montana, and Bob Marshall Wilderness areas in Montana by a noted storyteller, 160 pages, clothbound and softcover editions.*

Mules & Mountains, By Margie E. Hahn, *the story of Walt Hahn, Forest Service Packer, 164 pages, clothbound or softcover editions.*

Hunting Books

Hunting Wild Turkeys in the West, By John Higley. *The most comprehensive book done on this subject, recently updated, 154 pages, many photos, softcover.*

High Pressure Elk Hunting, By Mike Lapinski. *The latest book available on hunting elk that have become educated to the presence of more hunters working them, 192 pages, many photographs, hardcover or softcover.*

Bugling for Elk, By Dwight Schuh, *the bible on hunting early-season elk. A recognized classic, 164 pages, softcover edition only.*

Elk Hunting in the Northern Rockies, By Ed Wolff. *Uses expertise of five recognized elk hunting experts to show the five basic concepts used to hunt elk. Another of our very popular books, 162 pages, many photographs.*

The Woodsman and His Hatchet, By Bud Cheff, *Eighty years on back country survival by an expert whose secrets of common sense wilderness survival are described in detail, 112 pages, softcover only.*

Field Care Handbook For The Hunter & Fisherman, By Bill Sager & Duncan Gilchrist, *168 pages, comb binding, many photographs and illustrations. The most comprehensive field care handbook available.*

Hunting Open Country Mule Deer, By Dwight Schuh. *Simply the best and most detailed book ever done for getting in close to big mule deer. The ultimate mule deer book by a recognized master, 14 chapters, 180 pages.*

Radical Elk Hunting Strategies, By Mike Lapinski. *Takes over where other books on early-season elk hunting leave off to give advice on what the hunter must do to adapt to changing conditions. 162 pages, 70 photographs. Softcover or hardcover.*

STONEYDALE PRESS PUBLISHING COMPANY

523 Main Street • Box 188
Stevensville, Montana 59870
Phone: 406-777-2729
E-mail: stoneydale@montana.com
Website: www.stoneydale.com